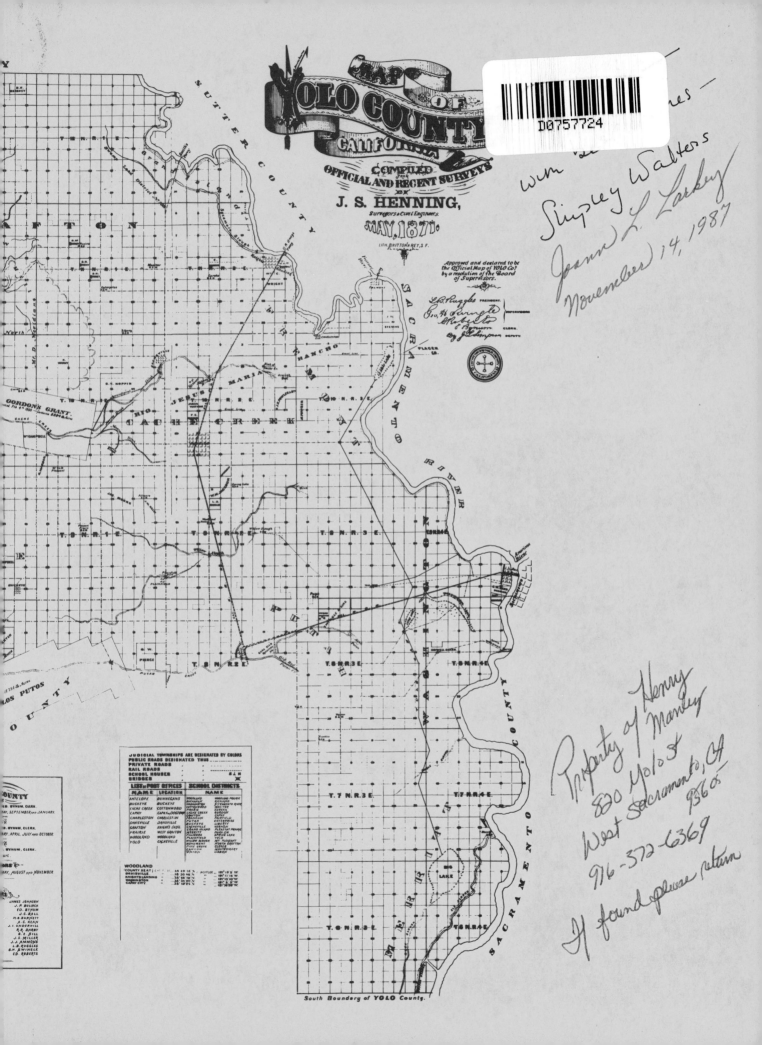

YOLO COUNTY

Partners in Progress by Marjorie Wellings

Produced in cooperation with the Yolo County Historical Society and the Yolo County Superintendent of Schools

Windsor Publications, Inc.
Northridge, California

YOLO COUNTY

LAND OF CHANGING PATTERNS

AN ILLUSTRATED HISTORY — BY JOANN L. LARKEY AND SHIPLEY WALTERS

To the record keepers, historians, researchers, chroniclers, and observers of human events—all those men and women who have contributed to the historical resources upon which this volume is based— we dedicate this history of Yolo County.

Right: The gang plow was used in Yolo County as early as 1854. One man and eight mules could cover the same area as fifty men with an ordinary plow. In the photograph, taken in the 1860s, George Hutton Swingle poses with a plow and team on his ranch east of present day Davis.

Previous page: The success of Davis Newcomer Hershey is reflected in this 1879 view of his family residence and ranch headquarters near Blacks (Zamora). This lithograph was drawn shortly after the railroad was extended through northern Yolo County. Hershey—a rancher, businessman, lawmaker, and civic leader —was renowned for his role in building the Woodland Opera House of 1896. From Frank T. Gilbert's The Illustrated Atlas and History of Yolo County, 1879. Courtesy, DePue and Company

Windsor Publications, Inc.—History Books Division
Vice-President of Publishing: Hal Silverman
Editorial Director: Teri Davis Greenberg
Design Director: Alexander D'Anca
Director, Corporate Biographies: Karen Story

Staff for *Land of Changing Patterns*
Editor: Marilyn Horn
Picture Editor: Laura Cordova
Assistant Director, Corporate Biographies: Phyllis Gray
Editor, Corporate Biographies: Brenda Berryhill
Production Editor, Corporate Biographies: Una FitzSimons
Editorial Assistants: Kathy M. Brown, Nina Kanga, Susan Kanga, Pat Pittman, Jeff Reeves
Proofreader: Susan Muhler
Layout Artist, Corporate Biographies: Mari Catherine Preimesberger
Sales Representative: Clair Freeman

Designer: Christina McKibbin

Library of Congress Cataloging-in-Publication Number 87-25417

CONTENTS

PREFACE

A comprehensive history of Yolo County could easily fill several thick volumes. Indeed, each period of the county's rich history and each community that was founded deserves a special volume. It was a challenge, therefore, to condense the county's history into a 136-page manuscript and select 130 appropriate photographs that often tell us more about the past and the present than mere words can convey.

The decision to dedicate this book to those who compiled the historical records that we consulted reflects our deep appreciation for their efforts. As authors, we have had the privilege of balancing the wealth of primary source material that is available today in archival collections and libraries, such as government records, newspaper files, and oral histories, with the information-packed but undocumented histories of Yolo County that were published in 1870, 1879, 1913, 1940, and 1967.

Our goal in writing this work about how Yolo County has been changed over time was to give readers a sense of place, an appreciation of the beauty of the land, and an understanding of the natural and human forces that shaped Yolo County's development. The contrasts between the natural environment of the Patwin, when one-third of the county was annually flooded, and the present era, when urban development encroaches on prime agricultural land, are dramatic. Yet this is basically a story of the people who came to live on the land, and whose cooperative or individual actions brought about change. The persevering pioneer spirit, the heritage of an earlier century, is still at work today as new challenges arise and are met.

The waters of Putah Creek west of Winters have attracted picnickers, swimmers, boaters, and fishermen through the years. Construction of a 15-foot percolation dam at Winters in 1937 backed up the waters of the creek to restore the area's ground water, and a summer recreation area was created. Courtesy, Alice Denny Whilstone

ACKNOWLEDGMENTS

In the preparation of this book many individuals and institutions gave us suggestions and encouragement, information and photographs. We are truly grateful for their help.

Many individuals assisted the research and writing of this book. We are particularly indebted to: Jack J. Potter, former Yolo County Schools superintendent, who suggested that we write an updated Yolo County history; the Yolo County Historical Society which enthusiastically cosponsored this project; Dr. W. Turrentine Jackson, professor of California History at UC Davis, who was helpful in his advice regarding sources and determining the scope of the book; and Dr. Joseph A. McGowan, an authority on Sacramento Valley history, who read the final manuscript for historical content.

We thank particularly the institutions in Yolo County: County Archives, Steve Webber, archivist; County Library, Mary Stephens, librarian; County Historical Museum, Monica Stengert, curator; County Superintendent of Schools, County Clerk/Recorder, and County Flood Control and Irrigation District; the historical collections of the Yolo County Historical Society, the cities of Davis, Winters, and Woodland, Friends of the East Yolo, Clarksburg, and Knights Landing libraries, West Sacramento Land Company, and River Garden Farms; and the Archives and Special Collections of the University Library, UC Davis.

We are also grateful for the help from institutions in Sacramento: The California Room of the State Library, California State Archives, California State Railroad Museum, Sacramento Museum and History Center, and U.S. Army Corps of Engineers library. And at UC Berkeley, the Bancroft Library and Lowie Museum of Anthropology.

We appreciate the generous loan of photographs from the private collections of Earl Balch, C.L. Eddy & Sons, Eleanor Emison, Mr. and Mrs. Charles Hardy, Harvey Hemenway, Ada Merhoff, Gladys Owens, Jack Potter, Jane Reiff, Don Urain, and Warren A. Westgate.

Lastly, but with great sincerity, we acknowledge special support and assistance fom Dick Larkey and Dick Walters; and Gerri Adler, Tom Anderson, John Brinley, Lynn Campbell, Betty Coman, Julius Feher, Ray Fisher, Suzanne Griset, Michael Harrison, David Herbst, Bob Heringer, Patti Johnson, Gregory Vasey, and Jack Weaver.   —Joann L. Larkey and Shipley Walters

The pride and joy of Woodland's Fire Department, Engine No. 1, is shown on parade in front of the first Woodland Opera House in 1888. The engine was purchased in 1876 and is still used in Woodland parades. The opera house opened on February 16, 1885, with a production of Shakespeare's Merchant of Venice. Until the opera house was destroyed by fire in 1892, it was the scene of plays, melodrama, farce, concerts, and lectures. Courtesy, Yolo County Historical Museum

This drawing depicts a small native village typical of those found along the Sacramento River by anthropologist Stephen Powers in 1876. Smoke rises from a hole in the center of these earth-covered semi-subterranean homes that were well suited to Northern California's climate. Inside, raised sleeping platforms encircled a central firepit, leaving living space for several related families. Each village had three communal structures: a ceremonial dance house, a sudatory or sweathouse, and a menstrual hut. Farther south and away from the river, homes were covered with layers of woven tules. From Tribes of California, *1877. Courtesy,* U.S. Department of the Interior

1

NATURE'S DESIGN: LAND OF THE PATWIN

PREHISTORY TO 1841

Gone are the Indian trails that were the first man-made patterns on the landscape of Yolo County. Modern freeways now arc across this land, carrying travelers through the western Sacramento Valley where rivers, sloughs, and flooded swamplands once barred both wayfarers and settlers. Those who came and stayed reclaimed and cultivated the land, established communities, and developed the county's agricultural and commercial resources.

The name "Yolo" was taken from the native Patwin word *yoloy* meaning "a place abounding with rushes." Yolo's boundaries were determined by natural features—the summit of the inner Coast Ranges on the west, the Sacramento River on the east, Putah Creek on the south, and an alignment with Sycamore Slough on the north. Subsequent boundary changes gave Yolo County its present landmass of 1,034 square miles. From the eastern boundary, the land increases in elevation from below sea level in the delta area to a height of 3,046 feet on the summit of Berryessa Peak in the western Blue Ridge Mountains.

The notched skyline of the Blue Ridge Mountains reveals the canyons of Putah and Cache creeks. Cache Creek, now the major source of surface irrigation and subterranean water supply in Yolo County, flows out of Clear Lake in Lake County. Putah Creek , which flows from the distant summit of Mount Cobb in Lake County, enters Yolo County

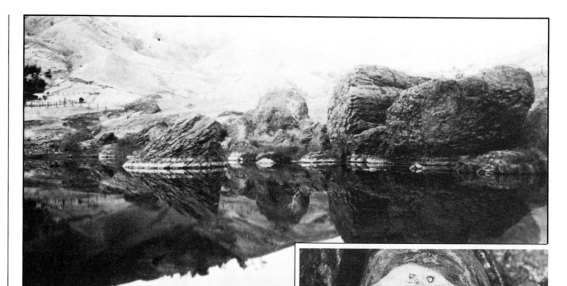

just below the rocky ridge called Devil's Gate where the Monticello Dam was constructed in 1957.

Through the millenia, winter runoff carried by streams and the Sacramento River deposited fine alluvial soils over an extended floodplain, creating sloughs and natural levees. Dramatic climatic changes occurred during the Ice Age, and during the cool, moist, interglacial periods, lakes and rivers abounded. Pine forests covered the foothill regions where oak woodlands now thrive, and mammals of immense size roamed the foothills and valleys.

Since the end of the Ice Age, this region's climate has been semiarid and new plant varieties have developed. The Blue Ridge Mountains were so named for the bluish cast of the blue oak woodlands and chaparral vegetation of the western hills. The valley floor supported large areas of open grasslands, while along the elevated borders of rivers and streams, dense riparian forests and occasional oak groves relieved the relatively level topography. Between the grasslands and the Sacramento River, seasonally flooded marshlands developed. In each of these areas, an inviting habitat for flora, fauna, and the first settlement evolved.

The first human inhabitants of the Sacramento Valley were descendants of peoples who migrated into North America from Asia across a land bridge that formed between Siberia and Alaska at various intervals during the Ice Age. Archaeological investigations in Yolo County suggest that human activity was present at least by 2,000 B.C. The Wintun people are believed to have intruded into the upper Sacramento Valley from the north about 1,500 years ago, and into the lower Sacramento Valley by A.D. 700. The name Patwin, derived from the Wintun word meaning "people," was first used in 1877 by Stephen Powers, an ethnographer working for the Smithsonian Institution, to describe these people who settled in the southern portion of the Sacramento River Valley.

The Patwin were nonagrarian, living in autonomous villages or groups of villages located on elevated ground close to a source of water. Each of these independent groups had a chief, a shaman who had ritualistic and healing powers, and a council of elders.

Located as they were at the crossroads of old Indian trails, the Patwin were able to trade extensively with neighboring Indian groups. They bartered for obsidian, marine shells, beads, salt, and hardwoods for bows, and gave in exchange flicker headbands, red woodpecker scalp belts, animal pelts, and salmon.

Old trade routes over the mountains, through Putah Creek and Cache Creek canyons, and between Indian settlements around Suisun Bay, were well traveled long before the first wagon roads were built. Other trails followed the Sacramento River, allowing the Patwin to trade with groups east of the river, providing access to ancestral fishing camps and to hunting grounds in the marshlands, and connecting the riverbank settlements. Patwin from far and near came to the river to procure fresh salmon, some of which was dried and ground into meal for later use.

Nature sufficiently provided for a relatively large native population. Oak woodlands furnished varieties of acorns—the staple of the Patwin diet. Roots of the tules were a significant food source for the River Patwin. Game was also abundant.

The massive grizzly bear was master of the smaller game animals who inhabited wooded areas. The grizzly was greatly feared by the Indians who did not hunt or eat them, but used their heads, claws, and hides in ceremonies.

The native people used the tall tule or bulrush stems of the *Scirpus acutus* and the *Scirpus californicus* in the construction of houses, storage structures, tule balsa boats, and duck decoys. Cured animal skins and pelts were woven or fashioned into bedding and winter clothing. Deer antler was used in making tools for flaking projectile points; the leg bones were fashioned as awls used for sewing and basket making. Skilled craftsmen

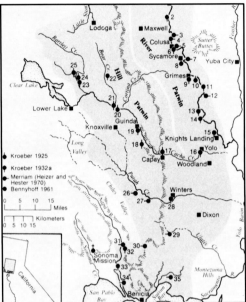

This map shows the extent of Patwin territory and locates village sites that have been researched by University of California anthropologists. At one time Patwin lived as far south as the Sacramento River Valley west of the river from the town of Princeton south to San Pablo and Suisun bays. From Handbook of North American Indians. *Courtesy, National Museum of Natural History, Smithsonian Institution*

used wood, stone, bone, and vegetable fibers to make bows and arrows, grindstones, harpoons, snares, netting, and other items used in hunting and fishing. Ceremonial whistles were carved from bird bones, while colorful bird feathers were intricately woven or sewn into special baskets and ceremonial regalia.

The Indians used controlled burning to encourage new plant growth and to manage the natural environment. In 1832 trapper John Work complained that the Indians had burned so much of the Sacramento Valley that "we can scarcely find enough feeding for our horses."

Glimpses of Patwin village life are found in the 1874 recollections of Isidora Filomena Solano. Born in 1784 in the village of Chuructos, located near the present town of Yolo, she was kidnapped by the Patwin chief of the Suisun Indians, Sem-Yeto (also called Francisco de Solano), and became one of his many wives. After they were converted to Christianity, they were married at the Sonoma mission. Speaking of the time after her abduction, she noted:

Before the arrival of the whites at Soscol we had plenty of very good food, without much work in obtaining it . . . My tribe, and many others, lived largely on fish . . .

Right: This old and mended Patwin cooking basket, into which pre-heated stones were placed, still contained fresh acorn mush when it was collected at the Kabby Rancheria north of Rumsey in 1904. The maker of this three-rod coiled basket called her intricate design "Loo-Look." It was made from redbud bark. Other useful household items pictured here include a whisk brush made of the soaproot plant and a bone awl used in basketry and for sewing.

Bottom, right: Coiled, slightly convex trays were an important form of Patwin basketry. Patwin basket weavers, principally women, were highly skilled artists who had a special knowledge about native plants. Baskets were used in almost all aspects of food gathering, preparation, serving, and storage. A tray such as the one pictured was generally used two or three times a day —for shaking acorn meal, winnowing fine particles, and parching seeds. This example was made of willow root and redbud over a single-rod foundation of willow shoots. The art is kept alive by native basket makers living in Yolo and Colusa counties. Courtesy, Kate Stephens Salisbury Collection, Yolo County Historical Museum

We had a great many pretty dances, men dancing with men and women with women. The men danced naked, but the women had a skirt after the white man came. Formerly, when there were only Indians here, the women wore only a collar for the neck, a crown of feathers on the head, a string of beads . . . wrapped around the body from the breast up as far as the neck. There was a belt of shells around the waist, while from the ears hung earrings made of feathers and beaks of geese and ducks.

A River Patwin village consisted of a cluster of semisubterranean, earth-covered, elliptical structures. In Yolo County the population of some of the larger Patwin settlements at the time of earliest record ranged from 400 to 1,500.

Warfare between groups did occur but was frequently settled by negotiation. However, a long-standing rivalry between Chief Solano and Zampay, chief of the Yolotoy, was still unsettled in the early 1830s, even after disruptive Hispanic influence extended into the lower Sacramento Valley.

Located in the interior of Northern California, the Patwin were untouched by Spain's colonial expansion into California until well after missions, presidios, and pueblos were established at San Francisco (in 1776) and Mission San Jose (in 1797). It was October 1808 when Gabriel Moraga, in command of 12 mounted Spanish soldiers and an Indian interpreter, led the first Spanish expedition into the Sacramento Valley. Moraga was directed to locate sites for missions and to report on rancherias, as the Spanish called the native villages. As he proceeded north from the San Joaquin Valley to the Feather River, Moraga made no reference to villages west of the Sacramento River in his report, but found the many Indians he met on the Feather River "to be completely hostile" initially. Although he found no suitable mission sites, he did succeed in exploring a huge area of the northern frontier.

Two years later, Moraga led a group of 16 soldiers on a punitive raid to a southern Patwin village of the "Suyusuyu" (Suisun) on the northern shores of San Pablo Bay. There, many natives died for the reported offense of killing mission Indians and other "depradations." News of this tragic encounter no doubt spread to inland villages. As a consequence, later exploring parties were either met by hostile natives or avoided completely.

The latter was the case when the first Spanish ships, the *San Raphael* and *San Jose*, sailed up the Sacramento River in May 1817 to reach a point in Yolo County above Elkhorn Slough. Those aboard were under the command of Father Narciso Durán and Lieutenant Luis Argüello. Father Ramon Abella accompanied them. After proceeding upstream against the spring flood for four days, Argüello wrote in his diary:

Suddenly we came upon a village on the west bank . . . We thought it might contain some people and with great care we went ashore. However, we found it empty of its inhabitants, for all without doubt had fled as soon as they saw us . . .

In the fall of 1821, an expedition made the first overland reconnaissance of the interior valley west of the Sacramento River. With Argüello in command and Father Blas Ordaz as chaplain, a force of 68 men with 235 horses was ferried across the Carquinez Straits and rode north through the land of the Patwin. The expedition's main purposes were to search for foreigners—Russian, British, or American—and to evaluate the Indian

Attired in the full regalia of a Spanish don, Luis Antonio Argüello posed astride his horse for this undated portrait in his family's collection. As commandante of the presidio of San Francisco, Argüello commanded expeditions that passed through what is now Yolo County in 1817 and again in 1821, after which he served as California's first native-born governor (1822-1825). Courtesy, Paul Elder and Company

menace. Included in the entourage were several Patwin neophytes who served as guides, and John Gilroy, a British sailor who had been in California since 1814. On October 23, Gilroy became the first English-speaking person to enter Yolo County when the party camped on the banks of Putah Creek near present-day Winters. In his diary, Father Ordaz described the rancheria of Libaytos as containing housing for 400 persons, although all but 50 were away "for the time to gather seeds." The Spaniards gave the name San Pedro to the river at Libaytos before proceeding north the next morning to the rancheria of Ehita (near Cache Creek). The expedition continued north as far as present-day Chico, then crossed over to the coast, and returned by way of Mission San Rafael. This epic 900-mile exploration was the last to be ordered by Spain before Mexico declared its independence in 1821 and a new government controlled Alta California.

California's last mission, San Francisco Solano, was established at Sonoma in 1823. It was built to secure Northern California against further encroachment from the foreign trading settlements on the California and Oregon coast and on the Columbia River. However, with an inadequate military force, the Mexican government could do no more than issue verbal protests. Foreign trade continued despite governmental restrictions, and American and British fur traders were able to extend their trapping operations into California's interior valleys.

In 1826 the legendary American Jedediah Strong Smith led a party of trappers to California by an overland route. Two years later, after Smith had been the first to cross the Sierra from west to east, Smith's party trapped up the east side of the Sacramento River, which Smith named the Buenaventura. Then he led his men up the north coast to the Columbia River. Following pathways first blazed by Smith and Peter Skene Ogden, British and American trappers forged a new trail over the Siskiyou Mountains between the upper Sacramento Valley and Oregon. After 1829 this route, basically that of present-day Interstate 5, was followed for the next 14 years by brigades of the Hudson's Bay Company that frequently passed through Yolo County in search of beaver and other furbearers.

In the spring of 1829, the first Hudson's Bay Company brigade entered the Sacramento Valley. This party of French Canadians was led south from Fort Vancouver by Alexander Roderick McLeod. They trapped down the east side of the river and spent the summer months in the San Joaquin and Sacramento delta. Crossing the Sacramento River in mid-September, they proceeded "westerly along D'Epatis River to the base of the western mountains . . ." Historian Dale Morgan takes this reference to mean Putah Creek, in the vicinity of present-day Winters. While encamped there they secured fresh horses from the Sonoma mission and were visited by the first Americans to enter the region. These included Abel Stearns, George Ayres, and George Washington, probably a black American who joined the trappers' brigade.

McLeod wrote of large numbers of Indians in the "Bonaventure Valley," with several villages of 1,500. On Putah Creek, however, he noted several villages where the ground was covered with bones. Asking his guests for an explanation, he was told that "punishment was inflicted on the natives by the people from the missions to subdue them to their Will and pleasure." Records show that at least 148 natives from Libaytos were baptized at the Sonoma mission between 1825 and 1834.

After leaving Putah Creek on October 8, the McLeod brigade traveled northwest to "another small river." (By 1832 this stream was called Rivière la Cache by the Hudson's Bay Company trappers because they had a cache or hiding place for their traps on its banks at French Camp.) In 1829 the trappers' route took them near the mouth of the Capay Valley before they returned to Fort Vancouver. The McLeod brigade set the pattern for other trapping parties to follow, and French Camp, located one mile downstream from the present town of Yolo, became a convenient rendezvous point in the Sacramento Valley.

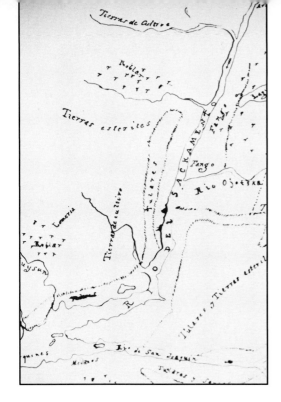

The foreign trappers had invaded the land of the Patwin and had disturbed their hunting grounds, but the greatest threat to the native people would be weather and disease in 1833 and a negotiated alliance made in 1836.

Severe floods during the winter of 1832-1833 forced natives from their low-lying villages, foiled trapping operations, and created mosquito-infested swamps. John Work's British trappers heading north on the Siskiyou Trail in the fall of 1833 passed Ewing Young and a group of American trappers who were returning to the Sacramento Valley. Both groups had suffered from "ague" and "intermittent fever," which seemed to abate when they reached the mountains. When Young's men reached the valley they found depopulated villages and the grim evidence of a major malaria epidemic that reduced the native population of the Central Valley by an estimated 75 percent.

The natives who survived this epidemic probably fled to the mountains, away from the flooded valley that bred the insect carriers of death. The survivors included a number of Yolotoy natives in the Knights Landing area who faced a new threat after 1835 when a Mexican garrison was established at Sonoma.

In 1836 Mariano G. Vallejo, commander of the Sonoma garrison, negotiated an alliance with Solano, the powerful Suisun chief. Solano agreed to commit no hostile acts against Mexican settlers in the Napa and Sonoma valleys in exchange for Vallejo's aid in subduing Solano's enemies, the Satiyomis,

Cainameros, and Yolotoy.

After 1836 Indian and Mexican troops participated in many campaigns against various groups of natives. Several were directed against the Yolotoy, ostensibly because their chief, Zampay, resisted the white man's intrusion and wished to replace Solano as chief. In June 1837 a military encounter resulted in the capture of Zampay and the relocation of his people to the San Pablo Bay area. Vallejo later recalled that Solano spared the life of his most feared and hated rival "so that he could have the pleasure of telling him every day that he was his savior." Zampay became a successful farmer after he and his people were exposed to a new way of life on Mexican ranchos.

Cattle and horses, trademarks of the Mexican rancho economy, were seen on the trails of the fur trappers by the late 1830s. Ewing Young drove the first cattle north through Yolo County in August 1837. After purchasing 800 head of mission cattle, he guided the herd up the west side of the Sacramento Valley and delivered 630 head to ranchers in the Willamette Valley. This cattle trail over the Siskiyous was used for many years to come.

The Hudson's Bay Company continued to send trapping brigades into the Sacramento Valley. Of the 16 so-called "Southern Parties" that were sent below the 42nd parallel between 1825 and 1843, more than half of them passed through Yolo County.

The explorers, missionaries, soldiers, and fur trappers of the 1820s and 1830s were the harbingers of great change in the Sacramento Valley. Yet they left no visible marks on Yolo County. Like the native Patwin, they used only the resources that nature provided. They did, however, nearly annihilate the native population through disease and relocation to mission settlements.

But a few Patwin survived. They reoccupied rancherias on the Sacramento River in the 1840s and one in the Capay Valley that still exists. Once resettled they adjusted to a new economy and contributed to the agricultural development of their ancestral lands.

The earliest known map of the Sacramento Valley is this manuscript diseño *in Spanish, drawn for American Captain John B.R. Cooper's request for land on the Russian-named "Rio Ojotska" (the American River). This section of the map locates Yolo County's principal waterways, Putah and Cache creeks, the flood plain and tule areas between them, oak woodlands (Roblar),* and *land suitable for cultivation. Cooper didn't settle in the valley, leaving land east of the Sacramento River available to John Sutter. Courtesy, California State Archives*

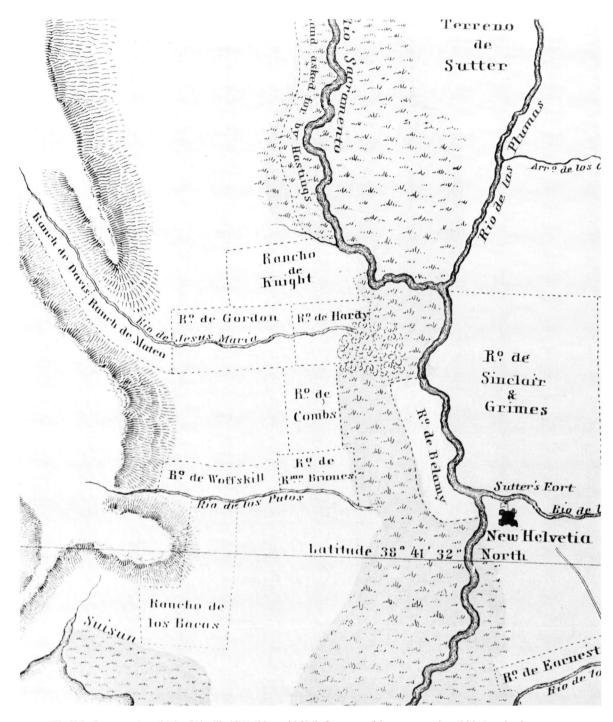

The Yolo County section of John Bidwell's 1844 "Mapa del Valle Sacramento" locates a number of Mexican land grants adjacent to the natural waterways. This tracing of Bidwell's map by Thomas O. Larkin, when it was published in Boston in 1848, was annotated with the first published location of the Gold Region on the "Rio de los Americanos." From The Maps of the California Gold Region, *1942. Courtesy, Carl I. Wheat Collection*

2

AMERICANS ON MEXICAN RANCHOS

1841 To 1848

The westward movement of Americans into Mexico's Sacramento Valley during the 1840s was stimulated by accounts of the region told by trappers, traders, and early explorers. Others were excited by letters from California written to friends in Missouri by John Marsh and Thomas O. Larkin. During the winter of 1840-1841, these letters were widely circulated in frontier settlements and some Eastern newspapers.

With Marsh's instructions as their guide, members of the Bartleson-Bidwell party headed their wagons west from Missouri in May 1841. Six months later, having abandoned their wagons east of the Sierra, the weary travelers reached Marsh's adobe home at the foot of Mount Diablo.

Meanwhile, the Workman-Rowland party, emigrating to California from New Mexico, set out over the southern route used by early trappers. This group, led by William Workman and John Rowland, traveled by pack train for two months to reach Mission San Gabriel in Los Angeles within days of the Bartleson-Bidwell party's arrival in the Central Valley. Members of five families who came to California in these two overland caravans settled on Mexican land grants in what is now Yolo County.

Some found a welcome refuge in John A. Sutter's fortified settlement on the east bank of the Sacramento River. Sutter, a Swiss adventurer, had arrived in the area in 1839 from Hawaii. With the help of native

Right: John Reid Wolfskill was a native Kentuckian who came to California in 1838. In 1842 he was the first settler in the Sacramento Valley to plant vineyards and fruit trees. He layed the foundation for the horticultural industry that is still flourishing in the vicinity of Winters where he located the Rancho Rio de los Putos, a Mexican land grant lying in both Yolo and Solano counties. From The Illustrated Atlas and History of Yolo County, *1879. Courtesy, DePue and Company*

Far right: William Gordon, a native of Ohio, established the first permanent settlement in Yolo County when he brought his family from New Mexico to a rancho on Cache Creek. Highly respected and hospitable to early travelers, he sponsored the first school in the county and had acquired large tracts of land in Yolo and Napa counties by the time this photo was taken in about 1860. He lived in Lake County for the last 10 years of his life. Courtesy, Julia E. Blythe

laborers, hired boatmen, vaqueros, trappers, and loyal Kanaka men and women he had brought with him from Honolulu, he built a self-sufficient empire. In June 1841 he received formal title to land—some 44,000 acres—which he named Neuva Helvetia.

New Helvetia had a sense of permanency about it when the first American exploring party arrived in August 1841. Commodore Charles Wilkes' U.S. naval expedition surveyed the Sacramento Valley and compiled a report on the natural resources, native people, and extent of Sutter's settlement. Wilkes' party toured California during a year of terrible drought and for the most part Wilkes' view of California was negative. He observed: "All agree that the middle and extensive portion of this country is destitute of the requisites for supplying the wants of man . . ."

By late 1841, however, the rains commenced and numerous members of the Bartleson-Bidwell party arrived, supplying New Helvetia with skilled labor and prospective settlers.

Sutter purchased the Russian American Fur company's property at Fort Ross and Bodega, and 3,500 head of Russian livestock—cattle, sheep, and horses. By year's end

Sutter's Fort had become the hub of settlement in the Sacramento Valley.

The first American to settle on a Mexican land grant in what is now Yolo County was John Reid Wolfskill who took possession of Rancho Rio de los Putos in July 1842. Two years earlier, he had selected the fertile and well-watered land bisected by Putah Creek in the vicinity of Winters.

Commandante Mariano G. Vallejo had refused to grant land to Wolfskill who never relinquished his American citizenship. Jacob Leese, Vallejo's American brother-in-law, interceded on Wolfskill's behalf and in May 1842 a grant of four leagues was made to Wolfskill's eldest brother William, a naturalized citizen who had lived in Los Angeles since 1831.

John Wolfskill bought cattle and horses for the new rancho. Branded with "96," these animals were his main source of income until grainfields were cultivated, and the vines and fruit trees he began planting in 1842 bore enough fruit for market.

Wolfskill was the founder of the horticultural industry in the Sacramento Valley. His cuttings and seeds had come from old mission gardens, his brother's rancho at Los Angeles, and George Yount's rancho in the

Napa Valley. He, in turn, gave cuttings to many newcomers, with the result that by the early 1850s vines and fig, olive, and fruit trees were growing on many of the earliest farms throughout the valley.

Wolfskill soon had neighbors. Thirty-two members of the Workman-Rowland party—the families of William Gordon, William Knight, Juan Manuel Vaca (Baca), and Juan Felipe Armijo (Pena)—were all settled on ranchos in the vicinity by mid-1843. William Gordon and his wife and seven children are said to have arrived at their rancho on Rio de Jesus Maria (Cache Creek) only a few weeks after Wolfskill took possession of his land.

William Gordon , a native of Ohio, had spent 19 years in New Mexico before moving his family to California. Even though Gordon was a naturalized citizen of Mexico with a native-born wife and family, he was granted only two of the eight leagues of land he requested in 1842. He petitioned for the land on both sides of Cache Creek, from the crest of the western hills to the Rio Sacramento. The *diseño* he submitted was named Quesesosi, meaning in Spanish "that which is solicited."

Gordon and his family moved onto their land in July 1842, and settled on a wooded knoll a half mile north of a convenient crossing on Cache Creek. With no immediate neighbors and no fences to delineate boundaries, the rancho's small size was of little concern to Gordon, who tended stock with the help of his teenaged sons and resumed his earlier occupation as hunter and trapper.

By early 1844, when Pierson Reading visited the Gordons, he recalled that there was "a substantial log house," and that Gordon had "yards, and a large number of cattle there." Historian H.H. Bancroft noted that "In '43-'46 his [Gordon's] place on Cache Cr. was a general rendezvous for settlers and hunters, and is oftener mentioned than any other place except Sutter's Fort and Sonoma." Bancroft described Gordon as "a rough, uneducated, honest, and hospitable man."

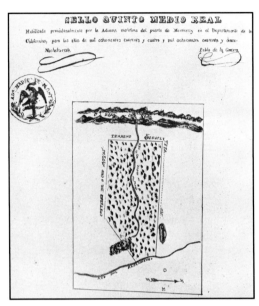

A year after the Gordons' arrival at Rancho Quesesosi, in the spring of 1843, William Knight, his wife Carmel Tapia y Arce, and their five young children arrived. Knight, a native of Baltimore, Maryland, had been in New Mexico from 1830 to 1841. Without receiving formal title to the land, Knight and his family settled on the former Yodoi rancheria site where the town of Knights Landing now stands. He called his land Rancho Carmel in honor of his wife.

In 1905 his eldest daughter, Mrs. John Snowball (Maria de la Luz, or Lucy), remembering the family's arrival said, "the bleached and dismembered remains of the former native inhabitants were so thick in the vicinity of the Yodo mound at Knights Landing, where Mr. Wm. Knight built his first rude house, that he collected and buried them in one side of the mound . . ." When the tule house burned several years later, a log house was built with the help of several neighbors. Here, three more children were born by 1848.

Knight put livestock on his land and operated a rope ferry for a time. He also cultivated about an acre of garden for the family. But being an active participant in military conflicts from 1845 to 1847, he was away from the rancho much of the time. Consequently, he made few additional improvements on the land before he was killed in 1849 at Knight's Ferry, where he had gone

The diseño, *or sketch map, of Rancho Quesesosi delineates the eight leagues of oak-studded land along Cache Creek that was requested from the government of Mexico in 1842 by William Gordon. Submitted with the initial request for a grant,* diseños *delineated boundaries, noted topographical features and existing native rancherias, and located new settlements. This copy of Gordon's original sketch, drawn by Francisco Arce in 1844 or 1845, bears California Governor Manuel Micheltorena's seal of registry. From* Designs on the Land; Diseños of California Ranchos and Their Makers, *1969. Courtesy, the Book Club of California*

to establish a crossing on the Stanislaus River.

Settlements were made on four additional Mexican grants along the Sacramento River in the 1840s.

The long, narrow island, bounded on the west by the original channel of Sycamore Slough north of present-day Knights Landing, comprised the 11-league grant made in 1844 to Manuel Jimeno of Monterey. Jimeno, who served as secretary of state to several California governors, soon sold his interest to Americans Thomas O. Larkin, John S. Missroon, and others. This densely wooded land, known as Grand Island by early travelers, was only sparsely settled at a few riverside clearings for many years.

Below Knight, opposite the outlet of the Feather River, Thomas M. Hardy, a Canadian carpenter and shipbuilder who had served in the Mexican navy, established himself in 1843 on a grant of six leagues he called Rancho Rio de Jesus Maria. Hardy was given all the land east of the Gordon grant along the Cache Creek corridor. He lived compatibly with a group of Patwin who occupied a rancheria near the crossing on the Sacramento River. Hardy raised stock from time to time, and with the help of men from New Helvetia planted a few garden crops. After Hardy's sudden death in 1849, his land was sold at auction.

Hardy's neighbor to the south was Jan Lows de Swart, also known as John Swartz. This Flemish immigrant had come overland with the Bartleson-Bidwell party, and in 1843 or 1844 took up land west of the Sacramento River. Having served in Governor Micheltorena's civil war of 1844-1845, Swart petitioned for a three-league grant he named Rancho Nueva Flandria. The rancho reputedly extended from a point opposite the American River outlet to the southern tip of what is now Merritt Island. By 1846 Swart had developed a settlement some six or eight miles below Sutter's Embarcadero where he caught, dried, and pickled salmon with the help of local natives. Before Swart died in 1849, he and his brother George cultivated vegetables for the growing population in the valley.

Rancho Five Leagues on the Sacramento River was claimed under Governor Micheltorena's general title of 1844 by Josefa Martinez and her husband William Mathews of San Jose. They, in turn, commissioned George W. Bellamy to sell some of the land to Joseph B. Chiles and others, but initiated no settlement themselves.

Inland, two of the last grants made under Mexican rule were Rancho Laguna de Santos Calle on Putah Creek east of Wolfskill, and Rancho Cañada de Capay on Cache Creek west of Gordon.

Rancho Laguna de Santos Calle was granted in December 1845 to Marcos Vaca and Victor Prudon. It was named by José de los Santos Berryessa, the alcalde of Sonoma, for the cold, elongated lake (Willow Slough) that then flowed from an underground spring about four miles north of Putah Creek. Vaca, who lived just south of the creek, later testified that "his cattle being used to the place, he asked for the grant of it." Prudon, Vallejo's military aide at Sonoma, got half of the 44,000-acre grant for doing the paperwork. The land where the city of Davis stands today was purchased from Vaca by Joseph B. Chiles who began putting his cattle there in 1849.

Rancho Cañada de Capay included a nine-league grant that was made in May 1846 to three brothers—Santiago, Nemicio (or Demesio), and Francisco Berryessa—who were veterans of military service at the presidio of San Francisco. Their grant extended along Cache Creek from the head of the Capay Valley to Gordon's rancho. They ran cattle there until 1847, when they sold their interest in the upper canyons to Jasper O'Farrell. O'Farrell, an absentee landowner, also established a large livestock operation in the valley. Jacob D. Hoppe, an American resident of San Jose, purchased the lower league and a half, effectively ending the Berryessas' interest in Yolo County.

These earliest settlers of Yolo County came for the prospect of free, available land, a healthful climate, and the chance for personal prosperity. Most of them settled comfortably into the traditional patterns of rancho life—learning the Spanish language and adopting the hospitable characteristics of the native Californians.

Although life was not always easy on the isolated ranchos, there were many happy social times. Round-ups, held in the spring and fall, and annual slaughterings called *matanzas* were invariably accompanied by fiestas. One man who had worked on the Gordon rancho in 1842 remembered that Sundays were always devoted to horse races.

The native Californians' horsemanship skills were admired by new arrivals from the United States, and the Hispanic system of branding livestock and using a 50- to 60-foot rawhide lariat was adopted by American cattlemen throughout the West. Peter Decker, passing Joseph B. Chiles' ranch on the west bank of the Sacramento River in 1850, noted that he had "seen Mexicans lassoo Spanish Cattle which they delight to do on horseback where they delight to be with a Lassoo."

Americans contributed to the livestock industry in California by importing purebred stock, particularly to improve the existing strains of the Spanish horse and the long-horned cattle.

Mission-trained Indians became an integral part of the rancho operations once secularization was completed in the mid-1840s. Then, according to Lucy Snowball's 1905 recollections, "permission was granted by the Mexican government to many . . . settlers to bring the Indians back to the places from which they had been taken. Mr. Knight brought to his grant 90 at one time."

Two revolutions and a war with the United States were to have grave consequences for those occupying Mexican land grants. Political unrest in Alta California, reflecting political upheavals in Mexico, was an accepted fact of life. But settlers in the Sacramento Valley were not greatly involved until late 1844, when José Castro and Juan Bautista Alvarado led a revolt against Mexico's appointee, Governor Micheltorena.

The governor looked for support from foreigners in the Sacramento Valley, prom-

ising final title to the land they had solicited. Sutter was commissioned to raise a force to march south. Joining him from across the river were Jan Swart, William Knight, Thomas Hardy, Marcos Vaca, and Ezekiel Merritt. Other newly arrived Americans in the Stevens-Murphy party were also pressed into service with promises of free land.

The outcome of this relatively bloodless revolt was the defeat of Micheltorena. On a battlefield near Los Angeles, kindred foreign elements in both camps had agreed not to fight after assurances were given that property rights would be upheld. Native-born Pio Pico was named governor and life returned to normal for a time.

Then rumors of war over the pending American annexation of Texas reached California. These were compounded by the arrival at Sutter's Fort in December 1845 of a heavily armed American topographical survey team under the command of Lieutenant John C. Frémont. Ostensibly a group of civilian "mountain men" that included Kit Carson and venturesome Jerome C. Davis, Frémont's expedition was treated with suspicion.

In early 1846, Governor Pio Pico lamented:

. . . We find ourselves suddenly threatened by hordes

Grizzly bears once roamed the hills and flatlands of Yolo County in great numbers. Considered a menace, they were hunted for their skins and their marketable meat which sold for a dollar a pound in 1850. Edward Wolfskill recalled that his father and William Gordon "would visit each other and make hunts for the grizzly bear," adding that "In this way they with others, killed and drove [them] away, until Old Grizzl was curiosity . . ." The last grizzly was killed locally in 1864. This circa-1855 drawing by Charles C. Nahl was modified by zoologists in 1953 to become the bear on the California state flag. Courtesy, California Academy of Sciences

of Yankee emigrants, who have already begun to flock into our country, and whose progress we cannot arrest. Already have the wagons of that perfidious people scaled the almost inaccessible summits of the Sierra Nevada, crossed the entire continent, and penetrated the fruitful valley of the Sacramento . . .

It also appeared that political rivalries between the northern and southern districts might plunge Alta California into civil war once again.

Other rumors that disturbed foreign settlers included the threatened expulsion of all foreigners, the possibility of intervention in California by France or Great Britain, and the "intolerable" prospect of thousands of Irish Catholics settling on a large land grant in the San Joaquin Valley that was provisionally granted to Father Eugene McNamara.

Particularly among the newest American immigrants, it was not difficult for Frémont to incite the patriotic and moral justification for the events of June 1846 known as the Bear Flag Revolt. Though he did not participate directly, Frémont later took full credit for promoting the theft of horses from the Mexican army, the unauthorized attack on Sonoma, the proclamation of the short-lived California Republic, and the taking of prisoners.

Participants in these dramatic events passed through Yolo County, but William Knight was the only grant holder who took part in the hostilities. Historian R.A. Thompson credits Carmel Knight for sharing with her husband a confidence given to her by Mexican Lieutenant Francisco Arce when he passed the Knight home with a small force of men and a band of some 200 horses. Arce reportedly told Carmel that General Castro would use these horses "to drive the Americans from the country." William Knight, in turn, rushed this intelligence to Frémont's camp. On June 10 a contingent of settlers under the command of ex-trapper Ezekiel Merritt took Arce's men by surprise and commandeered all but their riding horses.

Soon afterwards, a larger group left Frémont's camp, crossed the Sacramento River at Hardy's rancho, and proceeded up Cache Creek to William Gordon's. There, William L. Todd was recruited. (Both Gordon and Wolfskill, while sympathetic to American acquisition of California, refused to participate in this revolt.) The determined force then crossed to Putah Creek and reached Sonoma on the morning of June 14, traveling by way of the Berryessa, Pope, and Napa valleys.

After the defeat of Mexico in the Mexi-

John C. Frémont of the U.S. army issued this receipt for a $600 credit to Joseph B. Chiles at New Helvetia on March 23, 1844. The transaction indicates that Chiles, who had arrived in California for a second time in December 1843, may have provided livestock and supplies which Frémont needed for his destitute men who had just come over the snowbound Sierra. Courtesy, California State Library

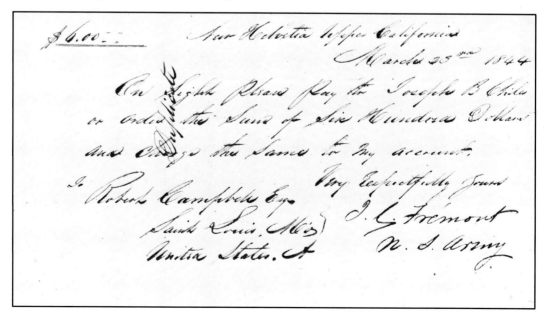

can-American War, peace was restored with the Treaty of Guadalupe Hidalgo of February 2, 1848, which granted California to the United States. A regrettable footnote to the American conquest of California was the U.S. government's disregard for the terms of the treaty guaranteeing protection of existing property rights. Bowing to pressure from squatters and land grabbers, Congress delayed action until 1852, when the U.S. Land Commission began reviewing titles to over 800 Spanish and Mexican land grants. Then, the grantees, or those to whom they had already sold land, were forced into lengthy and costly litigation to prove title to their lands.

Protracted court proceedings clouded land titles in Yolo County until the late 1860s. They also caused financial hardship for many, and created a climate of uncertainty and resentment.

Rejection of the titles to Ranchos Five Leagues, Five Leagues on the Sacramento River, Nueva Flandria, Laguna de Santos Calle, and Carmel placed additional land in the public domain. Titles were eventually confirmed for Ranchos Rio de los Putos, Quesesosi, Rio de Jesus Maria, Jimeno, and Cañada de Capay, and all prior land sales within their respective boundaries validated. Resolution of the Mexican land grant issue was a major stimulus to subdivision of large ranches and to the further development of agricultural lands.

Today, the imprint of several Mexican land grants are clearly visible on the land. The boundaries of Gordon's Rancho Quesesosi are traced by County Roads 94B, 19, 89, and State Highway 16, while Grant Avenue in the city of Winters and the old stair-step road toward Davis follow the northern boundary of the Wolfskill grant. Also, the angle of the original streets of the city of Davis are aligned with the east and west boundaries of Rancho Laguna de Santos Calle.

The era of Mexican land grants in Yolo County was brief, but the ranchos of the 1840s were the cornerstones of future settlement and the pastoral way of life and patterns of large-scale ranching were the era's legacy.

This rare photo is the only existing reproduction of the original flag of the California Republic that was raised after a group of Americans captured the Mexican headquarters at Sonoma on June 14, 1846. The hastily created banner incorporated the red star of the Texas Republic, the grizzly ("which always stands its ground"), and a red stripe, symbolic of the United States flag. William L. Todd, a nephew of Mary Todd Lincoln and a settler of Yolo County, designed this flag which was photographed in 1903. Courtesy, California State Library

The Buchanan Schoolhouse, located on the Knights Landing highway about six and a half miles north of Woodland, was typical of the one-room wooden schoolhouses that were built in the new county of Yolo. Courtesy, Yolo County Historical Museum

3

PATTERNS OF SETTLEMENT

1848 To 1868

Riders bearing samples of gold brought word of the discovery on the American River in January 1848, and the Gold Rush began.

The Gold Rush transformed California in two years from isolated wilderness to an American state. Yolo County was transformed, too, even though it had no goldfields. Instead travelers and settlers were attracted by its land and location.

One traveler who became a settler in Yolo County was Jonas Spect. Spect came to California in December 1847. After gold was discovered he was the first to prospect on the Yuba River, and he made enough money to set up a store in Sacramento to outfit miners. The next spring he loaded a ship with supplies and headed up the Sacramento River to found his own city on the west bank, opposite the mouth of the Feather River.

Spect chose that spot to avoid the tule swamps that lay between the American and Feather rivers on the east, and to take advantage of its location as the head of navigation to the northern mines. A sandbar blocked the mouth of the Feather, and all freight had to be unloaded there and carried to the other side.

Spect used the methods and labor of the nearby Patwin to establish a ferry across the Sacramento River. He staked a claim to 640 acres west of the Sacramento River in March 1849, apparently unaware that this area was part of the rancho granted to Thomas M. Hardy in 1843. (Hardy

Above: This high-sided Conestoga wagon, typical of the "prairie schooners" that brought so many emigrants to California, was driven across the plains in 1852 by John Bemmerly. His grandson Frederick B. Abele posed with the wagon in 1948 when the canvas top had been removed, showing how the vehicle had been adapted to farm use—for hauling freight, grain, and lumber. At other times the top was replaced for numerous historical parades. Courtesy, Yolo County Historical Museum

Right: Jonas Spect, the founder of Fremont, arrived in San Francisco at the time gold was discovered on the American River. On June 2, 1848, he made the first discovery of gold on the Yuba River, and the following April he and a group of miners drafted the first mining laws in California. From The Illustrated Atlas and History of Yolo County, 1879. Courtesy, DePue and Company

died in 1849.)

Spect formed a partnership with Thomas B. Winston to promote the town they named Fremont in honor of the famous pathfinder. A surveyor prepared a town plat and they began selling lots. By fall there were perhaps 700 people living in Fremont, and hundreds more passed through the bustling little town every day.

In the fall of 1849, Yolo, not yet a county, was under the jurisdiction of the alcalde of Sonoma, 55 miles to the west. The alcalde, who combined executive, legislative, and judicial functions in one office, governed a large district stretching from Sonoma to the Oregon border with the help of sub-alcaldes. On October 1, Fremont voters elected a sub-alcalde and a six-man council for their town.

On November 13, 1849, California voters ratified the state constitution and elected a state legislature. Yolo voters elected Jonas Spect as state senator from the district of Sonoma. Spect served as senator for only two weeks, during which time "Fremont" was suggested as the name for the county. When

votes from the whole district were recounted, it appeared that Mariano G. Vallejo had been elected instead, and he named the county Yolo.

The citizens of Fremont soon had more pressing problems to deal with. Unusually heavy rains which began in October caused the rivers to rise and wash away the all-important sandbar. By December boats were sailing up the Feather River to Marysville, and Fremont had lost its position as head of navigation.

Despite this blow, Fremont still expected to prosper because it was the only organized town in the county on December 15, 1849, when California's new state government began to function. The legislature divided California into 27 counties, each to be governed by an elected Court of Sessions that would serve both as a court and legislature. (The County Board of Supervisors did not come into existence until 1853. It then became the principal governing body of the county, exercising legislative and executive functions. The Court of Sessions was abolished in 1863, and its judicial functions were

carried on by the county court.) One of the original counties was Yolo, and Fremont's prosperity seemed assured when it was designated the county seat.

During the winter of 1849-1850, Fremont's population swelled to over 1,000 as discouraged miners came down from the cold, wet mountains. In the spring, Fremont dried out, county officials were elected, and the first post office in the county was established there

Above: John W. Snowball had this two-story Italianate Victorian mansion built facing the Sacramento River in 1877. There was no levee at that time, and the house was constructed in the delta style, with a large basement and elevated first floor that kept family belongings above the floodwaters. The house stands today behind the levee, south of the business district of Knights Landing. Courtesy, Yolo County Historical Museum

Left: John W. Snowball was a young English dandy when he came to California to seek his fortune. He was 25 years old when he came to Yolo County and established the first store in the community that was to become Knights Landing. Courtesy, California State Library

on April 9, 1850.

In June the three-man Court of Sessions held its first formal session in Fremont. This court divided the county into three townships: Fremont, Washington, and Cache Creek.

These political activities did little to improve the town's flood-damaged economy. During the summer people began moving away, not wanting to live through another wet winter. In August the Court of Sessions, sheriff, district attorney, and other elected officials moved to Washington. By October fewer than 250 residents were left. The county seat was moved to Washington in March 1851. By 1864 Fremont had so few residents that the post office was discontinued. Some of the wooden buildings were moved to other communities; time, rain, and floodwaters obliterated the rest.

Some who left Fremont moved upriver about 10 miles to Baltimore, the name of William Knight's settlement. Charles Frederick Reed was one. Reed was a West Point civil engineer who came to California in 1849 to look for gold. After settling briefly in Fremont, Reed was elected county surveyor in September 1851. He moved to Baltimore and married Knight's daughter Carmel in February 1853. That year he made a formal survey of Baltimore and laid out a town he named Knight's Landing. (The apostrophe was dropped from the name by 1900.)

Another energetic and well-educated man who moved to Knights Landing during this period was John W. Snowball, an Englishman who had come to California in 1850. After a short time in the goldfields, he opened a store in Sacramento. After his store burned down in November 1852, he moved on to Knights Landing and, with his partner John J. Perkins, established the first store in that community. In March 1853 Snowball married another daughter of Knight, Lucy Ann Knight Kendall, a 19-year-old widow.

The two brothers-in-law soon became wealthy farmers and highly respected citizens. Both were elected to public office and built imposing homes for their families in Knights Landing (Snowball's house by the river still stands today). They worked hard for their town, selling land to new settlers and encouraging new businesses. The official town plat was filed on August 17, 1870, and Knights Landing developed into the leading river port for the export of grain from central and northern Yolo County.

Another early settlement on the Sacramento River was Washington (now called Broderick), located in the northern corner of Swart's Nueva Flandria rancho. The town's first residents were the Kentuckian James McDowell, his wife Margaret, and their children, who settled on the riverbank opposite Sutter's Embarcadero in August 1847.

In 1848 Joseph Ballinger Chiles and his four teenaged children settled next to the McDowells, north of the American River. Chiles and his son-in-law Jerome C. Davis established a rope ferry across the Sacramento River near where the I Street Bridge is located today. Chiles and Davis operated the ferry until July 1850, when they lost their ferry license to Isaac Newton Hoag and William Carlyle.

McDowell was killed in a barroom brawl in Sacramento in May 1849, and Mrs. McDowell was left with five children to support. Although she could neither read nor write, she had 160 acres opposite Sacramento surveyed and a town plat prepared. In November 1849 she sold the first lot in the town she named Washington to August W. Kaye for $500. Washington's population in 1850 was 320—294 men and 26 women.

Washington was the county seat from 1851 until 1857, when voters elected to move the government to Cacheville (now Yolo), a small village on Cache Creek. Though the county seat was returned to Washington in 1860, devastating floods in the spring of 1862 led voters to move the county seat permanently to Woodland.

Travelers poured through Washington to and from the goldfields, crossing the Sacramento River on a bridge that was built in 1858. Businesspeople catered to the travelers' needs in hastily constructed saloons, hotels, blacksmith shops, livery stables, and laundries. The California Steam Navigation Company purchased one and a half lots on Levee Street in February 1859 and built a shipyard which became Washington's most important local business and continued in operation, under various names, for nearly 100 years.

The area also became known for its dairies. Jerome C. Davis established the first dairy in the county in 1849 near his ferry landing. By 1879 there were 13 dairies on the west bank of the river.

In 1864 Washington became the site of the first salmon cannery on the West Coast. The cannery—established by William, George, and Robert Hume and a tinsmith named Andrew S. Hapgood—processed 2,000 cases the first year. Twenty other fish canneries would be built along the Sacramento River in the next 30 years.

Left: Josiah Buckman Greene settled on Merritt Island in 1850. His diary of 1855 indicates what an industrious man Greene was, for in it he described how he, with the help of a man named Cole, worked his 600-acre ranch; did all the blacksmithing, setting of tires, and making of axles on wagons and buggies; made rat traps, a winding machine, an onion machine, and a seed planter; and did all the clock work for the entire community. Courtesy, Mrs. Curzon Kay

Below, left: The Varuna was the first steamship built in the Washington shipyard. Built in 1873 by the Sacramento Wood Company, it operated on the Sacramento River until 1907. This photograph, taken in the 1890s, shows a group of Southern Pacific boilermakers on an excursion. Courtesy, East Yolo Friends of the Library

The first person to settle on the west bank of the river in southern Yolo County was Frederick Babel, a 32-year-old German. In the spring of 1849 he acquired 169.88 acres of rich tule land about 10 miles south of Washington, at the mouth of the slough that now bears his name. There he raised horses and Durham cows.

Josiah Buckman Greene bought 500 acres of Merritt Island in January 1850. Greene soon brought his family out from Virginia and settled down. In the fall of 1852, he began building by hand a dirt levee reinforced with sycamore logs to keep the river from flowing through his home. This modest levee was the first to be built on the Yolo side of the Sacramento River.

Merritt Island and Clarksburg were both named for men who were not permanent residents of the area. Merritt Island was named for Ezekiel Merritt, one of the leaders of the Bear Flag Revolt of 1846. Clarksburg was named for Robert Christopher Clark, a lawyer from Kentucky who bought the site of Clarksburg in 1856.

Throughout the 1850s and 1860s, more

This 1889 photograph of J.B. Greene's home on "The Ding Ranch" on Merritt Island shows Mr. and Mrs. Greene standing in the front yard. The ranch received its name from a wooden sign that someone nailed on a nearby tree in 1852. The sign had originally read "BOARDING," but the first four letters had been broken off. Courtesy, Mrs. Curzon Kay

settlers arrived in the Clarksburg area. A school was built in 1856 and soon the town boasted a wharf, blacksmith shop, boardinghouse, creamery, and Chinese laundry. When Merritt Township was created in 1860, local voters elected a justice of the peace and a constable. By 1870 there were 480 people living in the area, and in 1876 the "Clarksburgh" post office was established. (The "h" was dropped from the name in 1893.)

In the late 1850s a settlement began to develop three miles upstream from Clarksburg. Called Lisbon, its settlers were mostly Portuguese who had emigrated from the Azores.

The first settler in the Lisbon District was Joseph Miller, an Azorean whaler who had changed his name from Joseph Souza Nevis Mello when he became a U.S. citizen. He arrived in California in July 1849, and in 1856 brought his family from the Azores to Yolo County. Two years later he bought 186 acres of swamp and overflowed land above Clarksburg, and began to farm with his wife

Josephine Paravagna and their children.

Miller encouraged a number of his friends and relatives to come to California. He helped them become U.S. citizens, buy land, market their produce, and start new businesses. Within 10 years dozens of small plots of land near Miller's property had been sold to Azoreans. Each plot had river frontage and a small two-story house, with living quarters upstairs away from the floodwaters. In May 1870 Miller helped organize the Lisbon School District, and he furnished the schoolhouse and paid the $400 salary of a Portuguese-speaking teacher.

Not all the newcomers to Yolo County settled along the river. Some settled on the flat, vacant lands in the interior of the county. They acquired land by gift, purchase, or theft; by preemption; or, after 1862, by homestead.

Settlers in the interior, finding dry, level plains with few running streams, began raising beef cattle. By 1855 there were 27,000 cattle in the county. But the flood of 1861 and the three years of drought that followed hurt

Left: Soto's saloon in the Lisbon District is pictured in the 1880s. The man in the center of the picture is the owner, Antone Soto, son of John Soto, one of the original Portuguese settlers in the district. The saloon dispensed refreshments to men and horses; no women were allowed inside. Courtesy, Frances Soto

Below: A crew harvests grain on the F.E. Collett ranch in western Yolo County in the 1870s. Steam-powered threshers were widely used in the county in the 1860s, and a portable steam engine for threshing machines was developed in the 1870s. These large machines were commonly moved from ranch to ranch during harvest time. Courtesy, Yolo County Historical Museum

many of the county's cattlemen.

The ever-resourceful farmers then increased their production of grain. Barley had been the first major grain crop grown in the county, with 126,076 bushels produced in 1852. Wheat became the county's dominant crop in the 1860s.

Farmers from the East and Midwest were discouraged by the hot, dry Yolo summers, but soon adapted to the rains which began in November and ended in May. They planted their grain in the fall and waited through the wet winters for the grain to mature. The hot summers proved to be a blessing, for grain and hay ripened quickly and wheat and barley could be stored uncovered outdoors.

The farmers' wives worked as hard as their husbands. Mrs. David H. Long, who grew up in northern Yolo County, wrote about the women she knew:

Above: This brick building was built in the late 1850s by William Gaston Hunt on his ranch on the south side of Cache Creek near Cacheville. Used as a Wells, Fargo & Co. Express office between 1861 and 1872, it was also a "drive-in bank." Large amounts of gold coins were brought here from the Woodland Racetrack in wagons which were unloaded inside the building to insure safety from bandits. Courtesy, Mrs. Paul Reiff

Right: This cemetery, located in the western hills of Yolo County, was established in the mid-1850s and was used by the early settlers in the Buckeye-Cottonwood area. Courtesy, Yolo County Historical Museum

Pioneer women started housekeeping in rude shelters with no floors, and cooked at a fireplace. The first stove in a neighborhood was an event and looked at with awe. There were no "fire 'pared" foods as now . . . All baking was done at home, butchering done, lard rendered, soap made, water heated for bathing and washing clothes, irons heated for ironing; all on the stove . . .

In 1850, 1,086 people lived in Yolo County,

mostly in the river settlements. By 1870 the population had grown to 9,899. Most of the growth occurred in the central and western parts of the county—near the roads and near the fords crossing Putah and Cache creeks. The first settlements in the interior of Yolo County lay along the road from Benicia, which crossed Putah Creek at Wolfskill's ranch near present-day Winters and proceeded northeast to Cache Creek.

About four miles north of the Solano County line, at Buckeye Creek, the road from Benicia divided, with one road heading north to Cache Creek and the other east to Sacramento. In 1854 J.P. Charles built a house for his family at the fork. Soon a boardinghouse and saloon were welcoming weary travelers.

Buckeye prospered as farmers built homes along the road and came to the little settlement for essential services. A post office was established there in May 1855. In 1858 the Wolfskill Rancho was subdivided into 21 large parcels on the north side of Putah Creek. The families who moved there were able to send their children to the new Buckeye School built in 1858. They also enjoyed lodge meetings, dances, and social gatherings in the new Masonic Hall. By 1870 there were 870 residents in the immediate vicinity of Buckeye.

The next settlement to develop along the Benicia-Colusa road north of Buckeye was

Cottonwood, named for Cottonwood Creek. In 1852 Charles Heinrich built a store and stagecoach stop three miles south of Cache Creek, near Gordon's rancho. The first post office in the central part of Yolo County was established there in March 1852. By 1870 Cottonwood was the service center for 1,319 people living on scattered farms between Cottonwood and Esparto.

A few miles north of Cottonwood a road branched off to the northwest, following Cache Creek into Capay Valley (named for the Indian word *capi*, meaning creek). In 1852 two brothers from Missouri, George D. and John D. Stephens, established the Oakdale Ranch along this road, south of Cache Creek and east of the valley's entrance, where they raised cattle and dry farmed grain. The brothers built an adobe granary which they converted in 1854 into a home that is still occupied by their descendants today.

In Capay Valley there were scattered houses along the road. Munchville, later called Capay City, was a collection of a few buildings, including Munch's store and blacksmith shop. Sylvannus Arnold and John Gillig purchased 16,700 acres of the Berryessa land grant in 1858, including the town of Munchville, and subdivided it into parcels. Gillig planted grapevines and fruit trees and sowed grain on his Adobe Ranch two miles northwest of the present town of Capay, and in 1860 he established there the county's earliest winery. The area developed slowly, despite increased traffic on the road generated in the 1860s when Charles F. Reed's quicksilver mine began operating in the hills to the west.

The main Benicia-Colusa road from Cottonwood followed Cache Creek until it crossed the creek at a natural ford about six miles northeast of Gordon's grant. A community known as Cochran's Crossing began to develop there in 1849 when Thomas Cochran established a crude hotel for travelers going to and from the northern mining districts. Cochran left the area in 1851, and James A. Hutton, who later became a prosperous farmer and county judge, acquired

some of his property. The Yolo Post Office was established there in February 1853, and soon a blacksmith shop and other businesses were catering to a growing number of farm families who settled in the vicinity.

In 1857 the town, now officially known as Cacheville, was formally laid out and became the Yolo County seat. The establishment of the *Yolo Democrat* newspaper that year was a sign of the town's growing maturity, as was the construction of a Union Church and a cemetery (later Mary's Chapel and Cemetery).

In 1860 Cache Creek Township, with Cacheville as its principal community, had a population of 1,995, the largest in the county. However, in September 1860 the county seat was moved back to Washington and efforts to locate the new Pacific Methodist College in the town failed. Cacheville stopped growing and settled comfortably into its role as the commercial and social center of the surrounding farming area.

The Benicia road continued north past Cache Creek, Oat Valley, the Dunnigan Hills, and Hungry Hollow, and on to Colusa. Many German families settled in the hilly districts in the 1850s and 1860s, raising grain and livestock. In 1856 those in the northernmost part of the county could get their mail at the Antelope post office three miles south of the Colusa County line. In 1855 A.W. Dunnigan and his partner Henry Yarrick had opened a hotel and blacksmith shop in the area, and with the addition of the post office the settlement developed into a commercial center.

Besides the Benicia-Colusa road, there were other roads for travelers during the county's early years, but they were passable only in dry weather. One road from Benicia crossed Putah Creek near Davis and proceeded eastward through the tules to Sacramento. A commercial center began to develop along this road when Joshua Bradstreet Tufts and his wife Mary, Forty-Niners who had operated a hotel in Washington, moved to the south bank of Putah Creek in 1855. They opened a combination hotel, store, stage stop, and blacksmith shop

that served the Davis, South Putah, and Tremont areas. They leased the property to William Dresbach, and the Solano Post Office opened in the hotel in 1862.

In the 1850s and 1860s, some of the finest farms in California were developed on the land north of Putah Creek, between Wolf-skill's rancho and the eastern tule lands. Here in 1851 C.I. Hutchinson and C.E. Greene began raising wheat, barley, hay, orchards, vineyards, vegetables, cattle, and horses on their 5,000-acre "Big Ranch." Jerome C. Davis and members of the related Chiles and Brown families began farming in the area in 1852. Davis' 12,000-acre stock farm received recognition from the California State Agricultural Society in 1858 as the most improved stock farm in the state. Members of the William and Alexander Montgomery families from Kentucky settled south of Putah Creek in the early 1850s and raised thoroughbred horses that became famous throughout the state.

Another road crossing the county ran west from Washington then headed northwest across the tules to Cache Creek and north to Colusa. This road crossed the two forks of the Benicia road, about six miles west of Washington. At the crossroads was the Tule House, where travelers could water their horses while enjoying refreshments at the bar. The Tule House was also the western terminus of the Yolo Plankroad Turnpike, a toll road built in 1855 four and a half miles across the tules. The Tule House was destroyed in the floods of 1852 and 1861, rebuilt twice, and finally surrendered to the tules in 1878.

South of Cache Creek, where the road from Sacramento crossed the road from Fremont, there was plenty of level land for the taking. The soil was fertile, wild game was plentiful, and the forests supplied ample firewood and lumber. Hardworking men and women cleared the land; planted crops; built homes and businesses, schools and churches; and developed the city of Woodland.

The John Morris family from Kentucky was the first to settle in Woodland. Two years after their arrival in Yolo County in November 1849, the Morrises settled on what is now the corner of First and Clover streets.

The Morrises had no close neighbors until 1853 when Henry Wyckoff settled a short distance away and built a store he called Yolo City. Wyckoff's customers were travelers on the road and settlers beginning to farm in the vicinity.

Yolo City might have developed into just another sleepy small town if it had not been for Frank S. Freeman. Freeman, a Missourian, came to California in 1849 when he was 17. He made $3,000 in the goldfields the first winter, then gave up mining for farming. In 1857 he came to Yolo City and bought Wyckoff's store. He preempted 160 acres of land bounded by what are now the railroad tracks, Main Street, College Street, and Beamer Street, and made plans for a town that he envisioned as a future trading center for one of the richest grain-growing counties in the nation.

The next year he married Gertrude Swain, who had come to Yolo County from Michigan in 1856 with her uncle and aunt, Mr. and Mrs. Clark Crocker, and had taught in a schoolhouse east of Yolo City. She was a strongwilled woman who wrote of her early life:

In 1858 I married Frank Freeman. The year previous he had bought the store in Woodland and sold liquor and merchandise. I said that I would not be supported by the sale of liquor, so he disposed of it. Cacheville was the county seat. There were no bridges and we had to ford the stream. The mail went through Yolo City to Cacheville and we had to go there to get it. Later a petition was gotten up for a post office and sent to Washington. The town had no legal name so I named it Woodland on account of the wooded country about.

Freeman promoted his town by building shops and businesses and selling them to merchants. The Woodland Post Office was established in July 1861, and Freeman was appointed postmaster. Freeman also secured the agency for Wells, Fargo & Company's Express, and in 1862 his efforts to have the county seat located in Woodland were successful. He filed a town plat in June 1863, and deeded a city block to the county on which an imposing courthouse was built.

Joshua Lawson, an elder of the Church of Christ, organized the first meeting of that church in 1854 on the Usual Shellhammer Ranch near Brown's Corner. In 1855 the congregation of the Church of Christ constructed a Union Church in what is now the Woodland Cemetery and the first school was built in 1853. By March 1861 Hesperian College, offering primary, college preparatory, and collegiate (or "finishing school") courses to teenage boys and girls, was opened at Woodland.

Two bridges were built in 1862 over Cache Creek on the roads to Cacheville and to Knights Landing, and traffic in and out of Woodland greatly increased. By the mid-1860s Woodland was well-established as the most important commercial center in the county. In addition to two county buildings, the courthouse, and county hospital, there was a steam flour mill, brewery, livery stable, two blacksmith shops, wagon shop, two hotels, drugstore, and six other stores, plus a newspaper. The former *Knight's Landing News* was moved to Woodland in 1864 and became the *Woodland News*. In 1867 the newspaper became the *Yolo County Democrat*, the ancestor of today's *Daily Democrat*.

The city was growing. New homes, a two-story schoolhouse, and two churches were built, many of brick from A. Hentz's brickyard. The town, which had first developed north of Main Street, began spreading south and west, in anticipation of the railroad that would arrive in 1869.

The railroad depot at Guinda was a busy place, especially during the fruit season of 1903 when this photo was taken. Empty fruit cars on a siding wait to be loaded. Standing with his family near the locomotive, holding his daughter, is R.L. Niemann, station agent at Guinda from 1895 until 1904, who later became a fruit packer and shipper and was the longtime manager of the Winters Dried Fruit Company. Courtesy, Craig S. Niemann

4

AGRICULTURE, RAILROADS, AND NEW PROSPERITY

1868 To 1900

By 1870 most of the arable land in Yolo County had been purchased, preempted, or homesteaded. Settlers arriving after the Gold Rush had farmed 160 acres or less, but in 1870 the average farm in the county was over 450 acres, and 69 farms were more than 1,000 acres.

In 1872 California farmers were required to build fences so their livestock wouldn't trample neighboring fields. Subsequently local farmers raised smaller herds of purebred beef cattle, brought in from the East and Midwest. Yolo dairymen improved their stock of prime dairy cows and sheepmen also imported purebred stock.

The demand for mutton increased dramatically between 1860 and 1866 after so many beef cattle perished during those years from floods and drought. Yolo sheepmen also made money from wool production.

Yolo farmers as early as the mid-1850s were also upgrading their hog stock. From the 1860s to 1900 between 10,000 and 20,000 hogs were raised each year.

Horses and mules were a vital part of Yolo County's economy in the nineteenth century. Stagecoach companies required hundreds of horses, and the development of gangplows and threshing machines further increased the demand for mules and work horses. Between 1860 and 1870 the number of horses in Yolo County increased from 3,940 to 9,773.

Organized horse races in the county were first held on the track

Andrew Work built outside Cottonwood in 1852. Three years later Carey Barney opened a track outside Knights Landing. For the next 50 years some of the fastest horses in California were trained and raced on that track. Racetracks were also built on the outskirts of Woodland, Davisville, and Winters.

At the same time, Yolo County was also gaining renown for its wheat crops. The county's soil, terrain, and climate were ideal for growing grain. In 1860 there were 13,236 acres planted to wheat; in 1863, during a drought, there were only 2,680 acres. Three years later farmers planted 47,705 acres in wheat, and increased their acreage steadily each year. By 1893 there were 231,306 acres of wheat.

Yolo farmers not only planted more wheat during this period, they improved their farming methods. In the 1850s the gangplow had made it possible for one man and eight horses to cover the same area as 50 men with ordinary plows. Horses and mules were commonly used to pull the gangplows through the 1890s, though plows powered by steam engines began to be used in Yolo County as early as the 1870s.

Machines that harvested the grain also improved the yield per acre and cut down on the need for human labor. Stationary threshing machines were used as early as 1851 in Yolo County. Since the machines were cumbersome and expensive, the grain from nearby farms was hauled to a central place to be threshed by one machine and one large crew of workers.

By the 1870s, growers were using "headers" to cut the grain heads from the stalks and mechanical feeders to feed the grain into threshers. By the 1880s combined harvesters, or "combines," were being manufactured in California. These machines combined "heading" and threshing in one steam-powered machine that was hauled from field to field. Once threshed, the wheat was sacked, loaded on wagons, and hauled to warehouses to await shipment by steamship or, after 1869, by railroad. As early as 1869 growers complained that speculators in San Francisco cut into the farmers' profits by keeping the costs of grain sacks and transportation high, and the price of wheat low. Farmers in the state formed the Farmers Union in 1871, which was replaced in 1873

by the Patrons of Husbandry, or the grange.

Eight granges were formed in Yolo County in 1873. That year their combined efforts reduced freight charges by 50 cents a ton and saved them over $37,000. They also cut costs by building a central warehouse at Davisville and by joining together to buy grain sacks. However, when Yolo farmers attempted to become their own shippers by buying a New York transportation company, the result was a disaster. The company failed, individual farmers lost a total of $679,000, and the grange lost its political clout.

More disaster was yet to come. Grain brokers had borrowed large sums of money to buy up large quantities of wheat, and had stored it in warehouses in California until the price of wheat on the European Exchange in Liverpool doubled. On August 3, 1887, the price of wheat dropped in one day from $2.15 to $1.35 per cental (hundredweight), and many grain brokers went bankrupt.

Despite financial losses, wheat acreage in the county doubled between 1880 and 1893. Though Yolo farmers continued to raise wheat, the "Wheat is King" era effectively ended in 1893, when a financial panic disrupted markets at home and abroad.

The other major grain crop grown since 1850 in Yolo County was barley. Between 1870 and 1900, 25,000 to 35,000 acres were planted to barley in Yolo County each year. The main buyers of Yolo's barley in the nineteenth century were beer makers in the United States and Europe. In English pubs particularly "Yolo Beer" was in great demand.

In 1861 John Scherley and Anton Miller started the Yolo Brewery near Woodland. They sold the brewery in 1881 to a group of local businessmen headed by Joseph Germeshausen, a German immigrant who had become a successful farmer in the Plainfield district. In 1879 there were three breweries in the county that produced 12,950 gallons of beer.

In addition to dry farming, Yolo farmers experimented with irrigation. Large-scale irrigation in Yolo County began in 1856 when

Here, a steam thresher is at work in the Dunnigan Hills of northern Yolo County in the 1880s. Farmers have cut the wheat and hauled it in small horse-drawn carts to a central place to be threshed. Note the chuck-wagon nearby and the tank for water. Soon, the stationary thresher would be replaced by combined harvester-threshers. Courtesy, Yolo County Historical Museum

Above: Double teams of horses or mules hauled as many as four connected grain wagons to centralized warehouse facilities that were built at various points along the railroads of Yolo County. This scene was photographed circa 1900 at the A.J. Plant warehouse in Davis. Courtesy, Yolo County Historical Museum

Right: Customers of Moore's Ditch, pictured circa 1900, purchased water that was diverted from Cache Creek into a series of canals and ditches. A farmer contracted to receive water on a specific date. When the water poured down the ditch next to his property, he opened his gates and flooded his entire field. Courtesy, Mr. and Mrs. Charles Hardy

Far right: Moore's Dam on Cache Creek, on the Gordon grant in central Yolo County, impounded water that irrigated thousands of acres of farmland for 50 years. The dam, shown here circa 1900, was also a favorite spot for Sunday outings. James Moore built his first brush and gravel dam here in 1856. Courtesy, Mr. and Mrs. Charles Hardy

James Moore, who had settled southeast of Gordon's grant in 1854, built a dam across Cache Creek. His first dam had to be rebuilt after every winter rain, and his first ditch was only three and a half miles long. But Moore's Ditch was widened and lengthened in 1864 until it irrigated nearly 15,000 acres of alfalfa and about 300 acres of grapevines.

More farmers organized ditch companies to get water in dry years. The first of many lawsuits pertaining to water rights involved the Cacheville Agricultural Ditch Company which built a canal diverting water from Cache Creek just upstream from Moore's Ditch in 1859.

In the 1870s alfalfa was the major irrigated crop in the county. Where farmers formerly cut one crop of alfalfa a year, now they cut five to seven. Moreover, irrigated land shot up in value. In 1879 farmland sold for $25 to $100 an acre; in 1900 grainland sold for $20 to $60 an acre, and irrigated land sold for $175 to $300 an acre.

Farmers experimenting with irrigation profited from the ideas of inventor Byron Jackson who moved to Yolo County in 1860 and lived on a farm near Woodland. In 1879 he moved to San Francisco and continued work on his most important invention—the centrifugal pump. In 1880 Jackson purchased 160 acres of land south of Woodland and

Above: In this circa-1920 photograph, alfalfa hay is loaded on a barge near Knights Landing for shipment down the Sacramento River to dairies as far away as Petaluma. In 1900 there were 40,000 acres of alfalfa grown in the county. Value of the crop that year was $984,115. Courtesy, River Garden Farms Company Collection, Yolo County Archives

Left: Alfalfa, used to feed livestock and enrich soil, has been a major crop in Yolo County since the 1870s. With irrigation a field may produce six crops of alfalfa a year. Courtesy, River Garden Farms Company Collection, Yolo County Archives

Right: Hops were grown along the Sacramento River from the 1870s to the 1930s. The sticky hop fruit, "cones" or "strobiles," were picked off the vines by hand and loaded into baskets. Hops were then hauled to a kiln to be dried and treated with sulphur before being shipped to breweries. Courtesy, C.L. Eddy & Sons Collection, Yolo County Archives

Below, right: Well water proved to be more reliable than ditch water for irrigating orchards in the 1890s. Here Byron Jackson (left), the inventor of the centrifugal pump, operates his new pump on his ranch south of Woodland. On the right is George Hecke, Jackson's ranch foreman, who purchased the ranch in 1909 and named it the Yolanda. In 1919 Hecke was appointed the first director of the California State Department of Agriculture. Courtesy, Mr. and Mrs. Charles Hardy

Facing page, bottom: Mr. and Mrs. Daniel A. Jackson are holding trays of table grapes for which they won the gold medal at the 1889 California State Fair. The Jacksons were natives of Ohio who moved to Woodland in 1864. They raised wheat on 80 acres of land east of town for 20 years before establishing their vineyard. Courtesy, Eleanor Emison Collection

developed the Yolanda Orchard where he used his new pump.

Irrigation made it possible for Yolo farmers to raise specialty crops profitably. In 1875 along the Sacramento River north of Washington, Reuben Merkley planted his first hop vines. Other farmers followed his example, and in 1878, 225 acres in this area produced 1,201,025 pounds of hops, almost half of California's total production.

Sugar beets were first grown in the 1880s, watered from the wells drilled by Herbert Coil on his farm northeast of Woodland. They became such a profitable crop that two sugar refineries were built in the county in the twentieth century.

Grapevines and fruit trees had been planted in Yolo County by the earliest settlers, but without irrigation they were not a significant factor in Yolo's economy. G.G. Briggs imported Muscatel grapes from Spain and in

Above: Picking, cutting, and drying fruit on the small fruit ranches at the turn of the century was an occasion for social gatherings, as the farm family was assisted by relatives and friends. This group gathered on the John Tilly ranch near Rumsey to process apricots in the early 1900s. Courtesy, Ada Merhoff

43

1880 was the first to use subirrigation by circulating water under pressure through perforated pipes. The first large raisin grower in California, Briggs eventually owned over 700 acres of vineyards in Solano and Yolo counties.

The best known raisin vineyard in Yolo County was situated near Woodland where the Yolo County Fairgrounds are today. Owner Russell B. Blowers planted his first vines in 1863, using Gordo Blanco cuttings. During the next 10 years Blowers produced raisins that won prizes in virtually every fair at which they were exhibited. In the U.S. Centennial Exposition in 1876, he received the award for the "best raisins in the world." The first to irrigate his vines by pumping and flooding, Blowers also invented the first successful raisin dryer.

Not all Yolo's vineyards produced raisins during this period. Some 3,700 acres, mostly in the Woodland area, were planted to wine grapes, and there were six wineries in the county. The largest wine-grape vineyard was the Orleans Hill Vineyard, located on 450 acres six miles west of Madison. Established in 1861 by Jacob Knauth, it was sold in 1881 to Arpad Haraszthy & Company.

In 1886 Haraszthy built a champagne winery on his property—a four-story building capable of storing 200,000 gallons of champagne. Unfortunately the hot climate made the grapes ripen too quickly to produce premium champagne, and the grapevine roots became infested with phylloxera. Haraszthy closed down the winery in 1899.

A surplus of wine grapes in the 1890s dropped prices for wine to as low as 10 cents a gallon, and a number of farmers tore out their grapevines and planted other specialty crops, particularly fruits and nuts. By 1891 approximately one-quarter of the land in the county was planted to orchards.

Many varieties of fruit trees were planted, and all did well. With the completion of the transcontinental railroad in 1869, Yolo County fruit began making its way to markets in the East. There, Yolo fruit commanded premium prices for its quality and because it ripened early.

Yolo fruit growers were active in the formation of the California Fruit Union in 1887. Russell B. Blowers of Woodland served as general manager, and Welester Treat of Davisville served as a director.

The union achieved an immediate reduction in freight rates that inspired other fruit growers to form their own organizations. The Davisville Almond Growers' Association and the Winters Dried Fruit Company, both founded in 1897, were notably successful.

The Davisville Almond Growers' Association, the first of its kind in the United States, established grades for quality control, purchased supplies at wholesale prices, procured labor at a fixed uniform wage, and marketed combined crops to the highest bidder. By increasing profits by four cents a pound, the association encouraged almond growers in other regions to form similar cooperatives.

The Winters Dried Fruit Company was organized to buy, sell, pack, and ship all types of dried fruits. Growers brought their sun-dried fruit to the company's facilities east of the Winters railroad depot for processing, packaging, storage, and shipment. During the first year of operation, 878,000 pounds of dried fruit passed through the company's warehouse.

The cooperative movement gave fruit and nut growers a voice in the marketing of their produce. Without their united efforts, they would have faced an unchallenged monopoly controlled by the railroad companies that provided the vital transportation links in the marketing system of the late nineteenth century.

* * *

The impact of railroad construction resulted in the development of new towns, the loss of a few existing communities, a general increase in the population, and greater diversification of locally grown agriculture products and commercial enterprises.

The Marysville and Benicia Railroad Company was formed in October 1852, with

Facing page: Russell B. Blowers of Woodland was awarded this diploma by the California State Board of Agriculture in 1871 for his superior grapes. Blowers was renowned for his Oil-Bleached Thompson Seedless raisins whose amber color was heightened by dipping in hot water mixed with olive oil. Courtesy, Fortieth District, Agricultural Association, Woodland

The five directors of the California Pacific Rail Road became the founders of Davisville when they formed the Davisville Land Company and began selling lots in their new town. (The town was named for the Jerome and Isaac Davis families, who sold 3,000 acres of their ranch to the California Pacific Rail Road Company in 1867 for $80,000.) On November 24, 1868, they officially recorded a 32-block town plat, bounded by present-day First, B, Fifth, and J streets, including the Davis Junction. They also donated lots for the Yolo School and three churches.

Rail service was completed from Vallejo to

Above: The first California Pacific Railroad train to stop at the Davis Junction, Yolo County's first depot, in August 1868 was the subject of this photo. Courtesy, Yolo County Historical Museum

Right: This 1890s photograph shows the Hugo Frommelt family on the porch of their saloon on Second Street between Margaret and Ann streets in Washington. Saloons were typically two-story buildings, with the bar downstairs and living quarters for the family upstairs. Though Washington remained an unincorporated community at the turn of the century, it had a few saloons and stores, a school and a town hall, an elected county supervisor to maintain the roads, and a constable to keep the peace. In October 1893 the town finally had its own post office, called Broderick after Senator David C. Broderick who apparently had no connection with the community. Courtesy, California State Library

J. Matthew Harbin, a large Yolo County landowner, as one of the directors. Though this line was not built for many years, surveying engineer D.B. Scott charted a practical north-south route for a railroad through central Yolo County.

In January 1865 the California Pacific Rail Road Company was incorporated to build a line from Vallejo to Sacramento that would intersect with the Central Pacific. Construction on this 60-mile main line was started in December 1866 and completed in January 1870. A 44-mile branch line was started in May 1869 and completed to Marysville in March 1870.

Davisville in August 1868. The town became a commercial center for the surrounding agricultural area, and by 1900 Davisville had about 700 residents.

During the late summer and fall of 1868, with the transcontinental line nearing completion, promoters of the California Pacific hastened to extend their railroad from Davisville, across the tule swamplands, to the west bank of the Sacramento River. Crews raced the clock to build the roadway and wooden trestles through Washington before winter rains set in.

Completion of the transcontinental railroad in 1869 impacted Washington's major business, the Washington Shipyard. By 1872 the California Steam Navigation Company, which owned the shipyard, was controlled by the Central Pacific, which sold the company and its shipyard to the Sacramento Wood Company.

In the spring of 1869, the California Pacific initiated its plan to extend a branch line north from Davisville to Marysville. Because of opposition of some property owners, the railroad took a long curve to enter Woodland on the west, over Railroad Avenue (now College Street).

When the first trains arrived in June 1869 Woodland had approximately 1,600 residents. The town boomed after that. Grain-brokerage firms multiplied, as did warehouses, flouring mills, farm-tool manufacturing plants, and blacksmith shops. Main Street bustled, and new homes, schools, churches, banks, and an opera house were built of brick instead of wood. In 1888 the *Pacific Coast Commercial Record* called Woodland the richest town in the U.S. in proportion to its population. Woodland became the first incorporated city of Yolo County in February 1871.

Once it reached Woodland, railroad construction continued to Marysville. California Pacific trains ran to the newly completed bridge over the Sacramento River at Knights Landing by mid-October 1869.

Knights Landing was a bustling river port with a population of 1,000 when the railroad came to town. The *Western Shore Gazetteer* in 1870 gave this picture of the town: "During the summer and fall months the streets of the town present a lively appearance. Long lines of freight wagons, loaded with grain, impart a business appearance that gives ample evidence of the wealth of the country adjoining. The flour and grain trade via the river is extensive, communication with the seaports being cheap and reliable at all seasons of the year."

The official town plat was filed in August 1870. The map showed the route of the railroad and a townsite of 14 blocks.

New businesses sprang up along Railroad Street as the town's focus shifted from the river to the railroad. The depot became the center of town, and several buildings were constructed near it during the next 10 years.

As long as the grain business thrived in Yolo County, Knights Landing prospered. In the early 1890s, however, when California wheat was no longer competitive on the world market, Knights Landing suffered. At the end of the century there were about 500 people living in Knights Landing and its heyday was over.

As railroad construction progressed, the demand rose for more roads to and from railheads. Dozens of new roads were laid out in areas of the county where settlement was increasing. These roads were thick with dust in summer and heavy with mud in winter, and many farmers in northern and western Yolo County looked forward to the development of more railroad lines. Their wishes would soon be granted.

In July 1875 the Northern Railway Company (a subsidiary of the Central Pacific which thwarted the California Pacific's plan for a competitive transcontinental line to Utah by taking control of it in August 1871) began grading a new line from Woodland to Red Bluff. At Cacheville the citizens eagerly awaited the arrival of the first train.

Over 3,000 people lived in the Cacheville district in 1870. The Methodist Episcopal Church, South, was built in 1867 which still stands, and a two-story schoolhouse was built

A fire called "Woodland's greatest calamity" broke out on July 1, 1892, near First Street and Dead Cat Alley. The blaze raced along Main Street, destroying everything in its path. The local fire department did its best, and reinforcements from Sacramento were brought in by train. The fire gutted two business blocks and one residential block, killed Fireman W.W. Porter, and caused $75,000 worth of damage. This picture, taken the next day, shows firemen resting beside the steamer, Engine No. 1, that pumped water to fight the blaze until it exploded. The steamer has been lovingly restored and is the pride of the Woodland Fire Department. Courtesy, Yolo County Historical Museum

Typical of small railroad towns, Blacks had its share of saloons among the eight business buildings, 13 residences, and six grain warehouses that were constructed within the town limits by the 1890s, when this photo was taken. A sign by the door advertises Yolo Lager Beer to prospective customers who pose by the hitching post and to thirsty farmworkers who might come into town after their six-day work week on ranches in the surrounding area. Courtesy, Jane Morris Reiff

in 1874. By 1891 there was a town hall on Front Street and an IOOF Hall north of the Methodist Church.

"Yolo" was used as the town's name as early as 1892. The post office had always been called Yolo, and after the railroad depot and freight office were given the same name to avoid shipping errors, Yolo was gradually adopted for the town name.

Surrounding the town, grainlands were converted to vineyards and fruit orchards in the 1880s. In 1890, 400 acres on Cache Creek, opposite Cacheville, were sold to the Yolo Orchard Company. Within a few years the entire parcel was planted with vineyards and fruit and nut trees.

The almost treeless area northwest of Cacheville was aptly called "The Prairie" by early settlers. Theodore Weyand and John Wolfrom both operated hotels, sold groceries, and alternated as postmasters of the Prairie Post Office that was established in March 1857 at "Weyand's Corners."

Religious services were often held in rural schoolhouses. The Prairie School served the United Brethren Church beginning in 1865. Members of the Methodist Episcopal Church, South, also worshipped at the Prairie schoolhouse from 1865 until 1893 when they built a church in Black's. Services for the German Catholics in the area were held in the Enterprise School until St. Agnes Catholic

Church (named for Mrs. Agnes Bemmerly who donated a site and funds for the church) was built in Black's in 1909.

West of Prairie, the hill districts of Oat and Bird valleys, Fairview, Hungry Hollow, and the Dunnigan Hills had attracted Protestant German settlers by the 1870s. These hardworking farmers welcomed the prospect of railroad transportation. Offers by James Jefferson Black and Anthony W. Dunnigan to donate a right-of-way and 10 acres of land for railroad facilities seem to have determined where the Northern Railway line would run.

Black, a farmer from Illinois, came to Yolo County in 1865 and acquired 160 acres of land in the Prairie District. He filed the plat for a four-block town he called "Blacks Station" in September 1875. Blacksmith C.H. Smart was the first to build a house there. After railroad service was opened to Black's Station in September 1876, additional stores, saloons, and residences were built. A seven-block townsite called "Black's Station" was filed in April 1877.

Grain was the principal crop of the area and the community's first warehouse was erected in 1876. Five more grain warehouses were constructed beside the railroad tracks before 1890.

By 1900 Black's had a population of 150. Gradual conversion of the surrounding grainlands to vineyards and orchards in the 1880s gave added stability to the local economy, but did not appreciably increase the sparse population. The town's name was arbitrarily changed from Black's to Zamora (after a town in western Spain) by railroad officials in 1906.

Seven miles northwest of Black's another townsite developed called Dunnigan. For 20 years, a small community called Antelope had existed there. In October 1876 the post office was renamed Dunnigan after Postmaster Anthony W. Dunnigan. The official map of the "Town of Dunnigan" was recorded on November 1, 1876, the same day rail service began.

By 1879 there were 14 business establishments in Dunnigan, a few scattered residences, a two-story town hall, a large stockyard, and two grain warehouses. The railroad built a depot and freight house, a section house for Chinese construction workers, a large water tank, and eventually extra sidings for the shipment of grain and livestock.

Although the town's population grew slowly from 121 in 1880 to 200 in 1900, residents of the area supported three fraternal lodges. An interdenominational Union Church was built in 1894 that is still in use.

The Northern Railway was important to Dunnigan's economy, but it was a different railroad company that would stimulate the growth of new communities developing in western Yolo County in the late 1870s.

An enterprising group of Solano County farmers and businessmen incorporated the Vaca Valley Railroad Company in April 1869. Two brothers, Andrew Muldro and George Bushrod Stevenson, gained a controlling interest in the Vaca Valley Railroad in 1870 and extended the line into Yolo County. They sought a share of the grain trade that could be hauled out of Berryessa Valley through Putah Canyon, or from southern Yolo County to their railhead on the north bank of Putah Creek.

The prospect of easier market access was well-received by the fruit, vegetable, and grain growers of southwestern Yolo County. In January 1875 a group of farmers and businessmen met at the Putah Creek resi-

dence of Theodore Winters and subscribed $30,000 to support the venture.

Theodore Winters sold the Stevensons 40 acres of his ranch for a townsite and consequently the railroad crossed into Yolo County just west of the Old Wolfskill Ford. Benjamin Ely, reluctant to have his home and ranch bisected by the railroad, donated a right-of-way and built a large warehouse four miles north of the creek when the railroad was extended along his western boundary in 1877. Hence, most of the people and buildings of Buckeye (which the railroad

Left: After the completion of the transcontinental railroad in 1869, many Chinese men like this one found work in the Sacramento Valley as houseboys or cooks. Clara Monroe Long, an early resident of Black's Station, recalled: "A permanent cook usually adopted the family and their interests as his own. He was interested and helpful in all their prosperity, broken-hearted in times of disaster, kind and mindful of the children . . . helped care for the sick, was generous with presents, and made it his business that all were well fed." Courtesy, Forrest A. Plant Family

Below, left: This 1879 lithograph depicts buildings in the town of Dunnigan and their relationship to the foothill district to the west. The earlier settlement of Antelope became the town of Dunnigan when the railroad passed along its western boundary in 1876. Before the advent of dining cars, train travelers stopped to take their meals at the hotel opposite the depot—25 cents for breakfast and 35 cents for lunch and dinner. From The Illustrated Atlas and History of Yolo County, 1879. Courtesy, DePue and Company

bypassed) were relocated to the new town called Winters. Winters received a post office in May 1875, when the one at Buckeye was discontinued.

G.B. Stevenson, president of the Vaca Valley Railroad, recorded the official "Map of the Town of Winters" on May 22, 1875. The 23-block townsite extended from Putah Creek to Grant Street, and from what is now Elliot to Third streets.

The official opening of the 12-mile extension of the Vaca Valley Railroad was the occasion for a special excursion to the new town of Winters on August 26, 1875. That day the editor of the *Solano Republican* noted, "The town at present contains 57 buildings of various kinds, and 30 or 40 more are projected and will be immediately built now that

lumber can be discharged on that side of the creek . . ."

One of these buildings was a Chinese laundry, for the railroad brought the first Asian community to Winters. Chinese men laid track and graded the Putah Canyon wagon road, and some remained in the area after these projects were completed.

Before 1876 residents had a two-room schoolhouse, a newspaper (the *Advocate*), a Methodist church, a cemetery, a brick community hall that still exists, a Granger's Warehouse, and 131 homes. By 1880 the population of Buckeye Township was 1,086, and Winters, with 523 persons, was the second-largest town in the county.

More of the large land holdings were broken up during the following two decades. Subdivision of the Wolfskill rancho brought a distinctive new look to the land as rows of fruit, nut, and grape cuttings were planted on the former grainfields. Roads penetrated the previously unbroken plain as a new era of prosperity began in the region known by the 1890s as the "Winters Fruit Belt."

Capital investment on ranches was matched by construction of commercial buildings in Winters—the Hotel DeVilbiss, a new Masonic Hall, and a refurbished Opera House on Main Street. Progressive citizens not only supported a local newspaper (the Winters *Express*, founded in 1884 by Edwin C. Rust and still serving the community) and the

Below: The 17-room hotel originally built at Madison in 1877 by L.W. Hilliker was operated by Lou Phansteel in the early 1890s when this photo was taken. Note the special entrance for ladies where a group of bouquet-carrying women are gathered, perhaps for a wedding feast. The Phansteel Hotel was one of a whole block of Madison buildings that were destroyed in a $25,000 fire on May 19, 1894. Courtesy, Lavinia Niemann Young

Right: Repair of major earthquake damage to brick and stone buildings in the Winters business district were well underway when local photographer Walter Hemenway recorded this scene on Main Street, soon after the area suffered a sequence of destructive earthquakes and aftershocks on April 19, 21, and 29, 1892, that were in the magnitude of 6.5, 6, and 5, respectively, on the Richter Scale. Within a month, however, Main Street was back to normal due to community cooperation. Courtesy, Harvey Hemenway

The elegant three-story Esparto Hotel, constructed in 1889 and pictured here circa 1900, was operated during the early years by Mr. and Mrs. Watson Barnes. It featured such modern conveniences as a pressurized water system, gas lights, electric bells, and speaking tubes. When Esparto and the Capay Valley populations did not increase as promoters hoped they would, the hotel went through a succession of owners and was eventually torn down in 1935 by Roy Wyatt. Courtesy, Yolo County Historical Museum

locally owned Bank of Winters (founded in 1885), but they established in 1892 the first high school in Yolo County. The City of Winters was incorporated on February 9, 1898.

The Vaca Valley and Clear Lake Railroad Company was incorporated in February 1877 to extend the line north from Winters to Cache Creek, through the Capay Valley, and on to Clear Lake. Most farmers in the area were eager to donate land for the railroad, but major property owners in Cottonwood refused to yield. So when Daniel Bradley Hurlbut generously offered to donate "$1,000 in cash, the right-of-way through his land, and 63 acres of his 844-acre ranch for a terminal townsite," the railroad directors accepted his offer. The tracks detoured around Cottonwood, and a new town Hurlbut called Madison after his hometown in Wisconsin was developed a mile and a half north of Cottonwood.

Cottonwood's Cache Creek Post Office was discontinued in 1877 in favor of the one at Madison. Many homes and businesses were moved to the new town, and today only shoemaker Abe Gostick's house and the

Cottonwood Cemetery mark western Yolo County's earliest community.

Hurlbut recorded the "Map of Madison" on January 22, 1877. A townsite of 19 blocks was laid out west of Railroad Street and south of Woodland Road. Madison quickly became an important center for the shipment of grain from the Capay Valley, the Fairview and lower Hungry Hollow districts, and the Gordon and Cottonwood townships.

By the end of 1877, the town had a large grain warehouse, a flour mill, a Christian church, and a short-lived newspaper, the *Herald.* The following year fraternal lodges and social groups met in the upper floor of Abraham Haines' store, and a second church was built by the Methodists. The Gordon School, established southeast of Madison in 1865, was subsequently moved into the new town.

In 1879 the Vaca Valley and Clear Lake Railroad received a contract to extract gravel from Cache Creek to ballast the California Pacific road from Batavia to its new terminus at Benicia. It was estimated that 10,000 to 15,000 carloads would be needed to shore up the new roadbed across the Suisun marsh-

Above: Mary Frances Nicholson Gaither, daughter of Missouri slaves, was trained as a nurse and practiced her profession in western Yolo County after she and her husband, August Gaither, joined relatives there in 1886. This highly respected woman worked under the direction of Dr. Thornton Craig, the Capay Valley's only resident physician. Beginning in 1890, she operated a convolescent hospital in her Esparto home for many years. Courtesy, Brenda Earl Jones

Right: This gathering under the deadfall of the Capay Saloon included the aproned German proprietor, Clemens Lautze, the town barber (right), and a group of prospective customers for the advertised Yolo Brewery Steam Beer. This saloon was built before 1879 when it was operated by Benjamin Dennis. For many years it was a favorite stopping place at the mouth of the Capay Valley. Courtesy, Yolo County Historical Museum

lands. Cache Creek gravel is still in demand, and the industry established over 100 years ago remains an important factor in Yolo County's economy.

The 24-mile extension of the Vaca Valley and Clear Lake Railroad from Madison to the head of the Capay Valley was delayed until May 1888. That month, the Vaca Valley line and seven other small California railroads were consolidated into the Northern Railway, a holding company of the Southern Pacific. The Vaca Valley and Clear Lake Railroad was allowed to keep its name, and, with financial backing from Southern Pacific assured, construction proceeded swiftly.

ager of the Capay Valley Land Company, named the streets and announced that the west side of town would be "dry." He sold the first 60 lots at a public auction held in June 1888. The town's name was changed to Esparto after a post office of that name was established in March 1890. (Esparto grass is a native bunch grass.)

An investment group called the Esparto Syndicate bought one half of the town lots and 1,000 surrounding acres for $100,000. During 1889 syndicate investors subdivided the farmland into 64 small tracts and made $125,000 worth of improvements in the town. The two-story grammar school also housed

The Capay Valley Land Company, a corporation of directors and officers of the Southern Pacific Company, purchased in 1887 "several large bodies of the choicest lands" in the valley through which the new railroad would pass. Purchases included the 1,380-acre Bonynge tract, and over 9,000 acres that were to be divided into five- to 20-acre tracts.

Developers of the tract formerly owned by Rhoada Stephens Bonynge located a new 580-lot town called Esperanza in the center of the subdivision. William H. Mills, the man-

the county's second high school when it was established in 1893, and the community soon had several churches.

The railroad was extended in June 1888 to Langville, a town that had been laid out in 1874 by John Lang and Jesse Aldrich. The Capay Valley Land Company had no lots to sell there and was reluctant to build even a depot until local landowners helped underwrite its construction. By 1889 a depot, section boss house, bunkhouse, and toolshed had been built, and the town's name changed to Capay. The community's population was

Members of the Methodist Episcopal Church of Guinda pose in front of their church, built in 1895 on a flat west of the county road. The only house of worship ever built in the Capay Valley, it eventually became the Guinda Methodist Community Church and was used until it was replaced by a new church building in 1960. Courtesy, Craig S. Niemann

augmented at various times by Chinese, Italian, and Greek immigrants.

The land company's plans for a community four miles west of Capay called Cadenasso—on land formerly owned by Nicola and Antoinetta Cadenasso—were short-lived. On the road six miles above Cadenasso was Tancred, named for a hero of the First Crusade. There, the Western Cooperative Colonization and Improvement Company was formed on June 5, 1890, enabling 41 urban families to procure 830 acres of foothill orchard lands on a cooperative basis. Principally from the East Bay Area, these families pooled their resources to plant fruit trees, hire a resident caretaker, build a Colony House, and develop a 60-acre nursery and park area that was communally owned.

Around this central commons was a townsite, where the Tancred Post Office operated from 1892 to 1932. A frost in the spring of 1896 killed many of the young fruit trees, forcing the company into bankruptcy and causing most of the cooperative owners to lose their lands. Subsequent landowners planted grain and hardier nut trees in this colder part of the valley, but Tancred never became a functioning town.

Five miles northwest of Tancred the 1,380-acre Guinda Colony Tract was laid out in 1887 on the west side of Cache Creek, including the 500-lot Guinda townsite. (Guinda is the Spanish word for the choke cherry tree that grew near the depot built in the center of the town.)

An influx of settlers in and around Guinda, and in the elevated Summit District northeast of Guinda where a number of black families established small ranches, caused the new town to prosper. The store built by Thomas Steele in 1891, still in use, served as a community hall until a town hall was built in 1909. The Guinda Hotel of 1893 stands opposite the depot site. The two-story Guinda

A Pomo woman, believed to be Daisy Hansen Lorenzo who lived at the Rumsey Rancheria, was photographed tending her children as she worked in the fruit harvest on the James P. Everett ranch at Guinda circa 1915. Her second husband, Harry Lorenzo, was for many years the highly respected chief of the Patwin-Wintun rancheria near Rumsey. Courtesy, Gloria Hamel Greeley

School that housed 60 students was built in 1892 and the Methodist Episcopal Church was built in 1895. Throughout the heyday of the fruit industry, Guinda had a relatively stable population of around 500 residents.

Rumsey, located four and a half miles northwest of Guinda, became the terminus of the Vaca Valley and Clear Lake Railroad when the line was completed on July 1, 1888. The 1,900-acre Smith and Rumsey Tract was named for the previous owners—four Smith brothers and Captain DeWitt C. Rumsey, who had settled at the head of the Capay Valley in 1869, on land he had purchased from William Gordon.

West of the creek, on a 925-acre townsite, the railroad company built a depot, a manually operated turntable, railroad sidings, a section house, and a 23-room hotel. The 1878 post office of Rock became the Rumsey Post Office in December 1888. The Rumsey School, built in 1891, was a center for religious and social activity until residents built a town hall in 1906.

Only a few homes were ever built within the town limits, but a number of fruit ranches were soon thriving in the district. By 1899 both the Earl and Buck Fruit companies extended their businesses at Vacaville and Winters to include packing and shipping facilities at Rumsey and Guinda.

Above Rumsey, on the north side of Cache Creek where Nicholas M. Lowrey purchased land in 1888, there still lived a group of about 100 Patwin-Wintun people who occupied an old village site. Lowrey and his family lived amicably with the Indians who lived under the leadership of a village chief and a council of elders. In this remote district, the native people preserved their traditions and religious practices. The Indian men and women worked on fruit ranches in the Capay Valley and sent their children to the Rumsey School.

The federal government purchased land for a rancheria west of Rumsey in 1907. Two years later, the Indians were reluctantly relocated to a site that had new wood frame dwellings but a poor water supply and little land suitable for cultivation. A number of Indian families moved to rancherias in Colusa County. Those who remained continued to earn a living by chopping wood in the hills or working on ranches in the valley.

The Vaca Valley and Clear Lake Railroad line ended at Rumsey although hopes for its extension to Clear Lake remained high until late 1890. However, failure of the Southern Pacific to acquire Clear Lake water rights, plus the high cost of constructing a railroad through the rugged canyon above Rumsey, resulted in abandonment of the proposed extension.

The population of the Capay Valley increased to 1,381 in 1900, but decreased during the next five decades. Trucking and the conversion of fruit orchards to less perishable crops gradually diminished the importance of the valley's railroad. The line from Rumsey to Capay closed in 1934, and from Capay to Esparto in 1941. Passenger service between Esparto and Elmira ceased in 1957 and the line was closed down 10 years later.

By 1975—100 years after the Vaca Valley Railroad first reached Yolo County—the rails were removed. Today only traces of the historic roadbed remain.

The two-week Pullman Workers Strike of 1894, the first national labor action affecting California, which halted all trains, turned violent on July 11 when strikers dynamited a railroad trestle in east Yolo County. The resulting disaster, shown in this photo, caused the death of engineer Sam Clark and four soldiers sent to guard a train from Sacramento to San Francisco. These deaths broke the momentum of the strike and led to sensational trials for the six accused culprits, all held in Yolo County. Courtesy, Mrs. John O. Rowe

No one appreciated the need for better road conditions more than these two brothers from Winters, Frank and A.B. Wilson, who made an epic 251-mile journey to San Jose on their high wheelers in 1891. The route of their excursion, by way of Stockton, with a side trip to the Lick Observatory atop Mount Hamilton and a return through San Francisco, was made part way by train because of flooded rivers and recurring breakdowns. Courtesy, Craig S. Niemann Family

5

DRAMATIC CHANGES IN THE NEW CENTURY

1900-1920

The first two decades of the twentieth century were a time of optimism and reform throughout America. In Yolo County this era of public concern brought forth new types of organizations as Yoloans cooperated to improve their communities.

One such organization was the multi-county Sacramento Valley Development Association. In 1900 in Oroville, nine counties formally organized the association "for betterment of their conditions, river improvement, drainage, conservation of forests on their borders and the advertising of their resources." Twelve counties eventually joined the organization, which lobbied for a system of state highways and promoted Yolo County as the most suitable location for a University State Farm. It also advocated the establishment of boards of trade or chambers of commerce in each community.

A chamber of commerce was organized in Woodland in 1900. Led by attorney Charles W. Thomas, this group had as one of its chief goals the establishment of a state school of practical agricultural education in Yolo County.

The new century also saw the formation of women's improvement clubs. The Woodland Women's Improvement Club was organized in 1902 with Miss Carrie Blowers as president. This club raised money and contributed labor to support a cemetery and a library, and its members participated in the annual Fourth of July parades. The club's principal goal was a city park. Members worked for seven years to purchase the block bounded by Oak, Cross, Walnut, and Cleveland streets which they deeded to the city in 1909 for the development of City Park.

A board of trade and a women's improvement club were organized in Winters in 1902. While the men engaged in promotional work, the women raised funds for street beautification and for their long-term goal —construction of a town hall. The land on which the city's fire alarm tower and the city hall were built was purchased with a donation from the improvement club. An additional donation of $1,141 was made to the city park fund in 1914.

Similar groups were organized elsewhere in the county, including Davisville, where the desire to promote their town as a site for the University State Farm prompted Davisville citizens to organize a chamber of commerce and the Davisville Women's Improvement Club in 1905.

The University of California, Davis, developed from a grassroots movement to improve agricultural education that took shape in the late nineteenth century. By the 1880s California farmers were becoming increasingly aware of the lack of practical training and research at the Berkeley campus, which had little land available for experimentation. During this period Hugh M. LaRue, a Yolo County farmer who was president of the California State Agricultural Society, and the California State Grange both advanced proposals for a separate agricultural school. By the early 1900s the idea of a State Farm had widespread public support.

A University State Farm bill was drafted in 1904 by Peter J. Shields, executive secretary of the California State Agricultural Society, with the assistance of E.W. Major, a University of California instructor. Two previous bills introduced by Yolo County legislators were rejected as being too specialized. During the hearing process, a delegation from Yolo County made sure that a rider was attached prescribing selection of a site with optimum land qualifications and an established irrigation system. The bill was unanimously passed and immediately signed into law by Governor George C. Pardee on March 18, 1905.

The University State Farm remained under the jurisdiction of the Regents of the University of California and the College of Agriculture. Its original curriculum was to include practical agricultural instruction for degree students from Berkeley, a three-year Farm School course open to boys 15 years old and older, and an annual series of Short Courses on farming for men and women. Research on specific problems was to be conducted in conjunction with the Agricultural Experiment Station and the U.S. Department of Agriculture. The bill also created a University Farm Commission, charged with the responsibility of selecting a site for the farm.

A full year passed before the final decision was made to locate the farm on a site adjacent to the town of Davisville. More than 70 sites in various parts of California were considered, but by January 1906 the choice had narrowed to four, including two in Yolo County: the Mullens Station tract a mile south of Woodland; and the Sparks-Hamel-Wright tract at Davisville. Professor Edward J. Wickson, dean of the College of Agriculture, was asked to evaluate each site. After a final tour of inspection, the commission members voted unanimously on April 5, 1906, to accept the site offered by the Davisville Chamber of Commerce. Davisville's accessibility by rail to Berkeley, the state capital, and all parts of California was a key factor in its selection. Thirteen trains stopped each day at the Davis Depot—a convenience for nonresident instructors who would commute from Berkeley.

Once the decision was announced, Davisites celebrated by flying flags and shooting off fireworks. The entire county shared in their success.

George Pierce attended to transferring the ownership of the 778.6-acre farm site from the previous owners—Martin V. Sparks, Henry H. Hamel, and Orin H. Wright—to the Regents of the University of California. He also

Left: The changing landscape of the Davisville area in 1910 is documented in this view of the University Farm, looking northeast. In the foreground are some of the earliest campus buildings. In the center looms the Davisville Grammar School, and oak-studded grainfields lie beyond the town limits. The leafless fig trees on the campus were planted by Jerome Davis in the 1850s. Courtesy, Special Collections Department, University Library, UC Davis

Below, left: Men and women attending the Farmer's Institute, held at the University Farm in October 1908, head for a lunch break after the first morning session in which they heard prominent agricultural educators speak about modern farming techniques. Courtesy, Special Collections Department, University Library, UC Davis

purchased from the Yolo Consolidated Water Company (with $3,895 donated by 78 Davisville citizens) and deeded to the university the water rights for the irrigation ditch that Sparks had extended to his ranch. Finally, in August 1906, after the titles were cleared and the state had paid $103,290 for the three properties, Pierce wrote in his daily journal: "Closed the University Farm deal by advancing tax money myself."

The work of transforming a fenced grainfield—with only a few old vineyards, fruit and nut trees, and farm buildings—into a model farm school got underway immediately under the supervision of professors at Berkeley. John Rogers became farm foreman, the first university employee at Davis.

During the months that followed, plans were made for buildings, road development, and operational costs. Construction began in late 1906 on a creamery-administration building, an octagonal livestock judging pavilion that served as a classroom and auditorium, and cottages for the creamery manager and the resident administrator.

The University State Farm was officially dedicated on October 29, 1907, during a three-day Farmer's Institute with attendees from all over the state. An additional appropriation of $132,000 in 1907 provided for more buildings, laboratory equipment, and a series of five Short Courses that brought the first students to the campus in the fall of 1908. One hundred fifteen men and women en-

Above: Statewide programs of agricultural education were under the direction of these three gentlemen in 1915, when this photograph was taken of (left to right) Bertram H. Crocheron, founder and director of the Agricultural Extension Service in California (1913-1946); Hubert E. VanNorman, resident dean of the University Farm at Davis (1913-1919); and Dr. Thomas F. Hunt, dean of the UC College of Agriculture (1912-1924). Courtesy, Special Collections Department, University Library, UC Davis

Right: Location of the University Farm at Davisville in 1906 generated an ongoing need for more housing. The well that is being bored in this 1913 photo still serves the city on a site that is northwest of Sixth and E streets, in what was then C.W. Bowers' addition to the town limits. Courtesy, Forrest A. Plant Family

rolled in these courses that lasted from one to eight weeks.

The three-year University Farm School opened January 5, 1909, with an enrollment of 18, plus five degree students from the College of Agriculture at Berkeley. Two years later enrollment had grown to 95, and there were 22 wooden shingled buildings situated on the campus' tree-lined avenues, and several experimental agricultural plots in the surrounding fields.

Faculty and curriculum increased gradually, with student enrollment remaining under 350 until after World War I. It wasn't until the early 1920s when a four-year degree curriculum and a building plan were adopted

that the University Farm gained a sense of permanency.

Farmers in Yolo and Solano counties made their fields, orchards, vineyards, and livestock herds available for student instruction and experimentation, and in return took advantage of the educational opportunities that were offered. Their agricultural operations prospered from the knowledge gained in the classroom and through scientific experiments.

Davisville felt the greatest impact of the new agricultural school. Only nine days after the University State Farm was located at Davisville, the editor of the Davisville *Enterprise* dropped the "ville" from the masthead of his newspaper, saying the town was no longer "a countryside place of insignificant import." The town's name was officially changed when the City of Davis was incorporated on March 28, 1917.

"We Are Growing" became the slogan of the chamber of commerce in 1906. Davis' boundaries were extended west of A Street to the campus (the Sheffer, Fairview, and Haussler additions), and two blocks north of what is now Fifth Street (the Bowers Addition). In 1913 T.G. Schmeiser expanded his agricultural machinery plant and organized the town's first waterworks, and the two-story brick Bank of Davis went up opposite the new railroad depot and signal tower. The influx of university staff created a demand for addi-

tional housing within the town that continued as the campus developed. The shortage was partially solved in 1914 when the first bungalow-style tract homes were built in the Bowers Addition.

Davis' nine saloon keepers suffered from the University Farm's location in 1906, as temperance advocates campaigned to close the saloons to protect the "farm boy" students. A law was passed in 1911 barring sales of wine and liquor within three miles of the campus. This ban was not lifted until 1979.

The people of Yolo County were the first in the Sacramento Valley to sponsor new programs such as the Agricultural Extension Service, organized by B.H. Crocheron in 1914, and the high school agricultural clubs that developed into the Future Farmers of America and 4-H clubs. These programs were funded by federal, state, and local governments and were implemented locally through the College of Agriculture of the University of California. The Agricultural Extension Service, planned and vigorously promoted by Crocheron, provided Yolo County with a university-trained and salaried farm advisor in 1914, after the board of supervisors agreed to underwrite $2,000 for his annual expenses and farmers in the county organized a farm bureau to assist the advisor.

Yoloans formed the Yolo County Farm Bureau during an all-day picnic held at the Yolo Town Hall on March 7, 1914. Dr. M.O. Wyatt, a Winters dentist with real estate, banking, and farming experience, was elected president. Sixty-four members signed the charter roll that day. When the bureau's first annual Harvest Festival was held at the Woodland Armory the following October, 270 members had paid their dues of $1.50. The next year a crowd of 2,000 attended the second Harvest Festival, held at Esparto in conjunction with the first Almond Festival.

Niles Searles served as the first Yolo County farm advisor from 1914 to 1919. His annual report of 1915 stated that within the first 18 months of his arrival, 11 farm bureau centers had been organized throughout the county.

FARMERS' PICNIC
(Organization of Farm Bureau)
AT YOLO
Saturday, All Day, March 7th, 1914
PROGRAM
MORNING
10:00—Music—Winters brass band—20 pieces
10:30—Meeting called to order by J. E. Scarlett of Yolo—Election of Temporary Chairman and Secretary.
10:40—"The Reason" M. H. Stitt, of Guinda.
    Outline of work and adoption of Farm bureau constitution; conducted by Prof. B. H. Crocheron, of Washington, D. C.
11:15—"How to Judge a Dairy Cow;" Demonstration with a live cow on the stage, by Dean Van Norman, of the University Farm School, who is also President National Dairymen's Association.
11:45—Address, Judge Peter J. Shields, Superior Court, Sacramento.
    Recess until 1:30 P. M. Old fashioned picnic. Bring your baskets. Hot coffee, cream and sugar will be served by the ladies of Yolo. (A chicken dinner will be served those who do not bring lunch, for a small fee.)
AFTERNOON
1:00—Music by the band.
1:30—Address, Prof. Crocheron; U. S. Agricultural Department, Washington, D. C.; "The Duty of the Farm Adviser."
2:00—Election of officers of Yolo County Farm Bureau.
2:15—Address, Chas. W. Shaw, University of California, Berkeley.
2:45—Address, "Yolo County's Highway Problem" by Chas. F. Stern, Member California Highway Commission.
    Every arrangement is being made for the comfort of guests while at Yolo. There will be good music, good speaking and a general good time for every person who attends.
    Bring your basket, well filled; bring the family and tell your neighbor about it.
LET'S ALL GO
To Yolo, Saturday, March 7th, All Day, 1914

During the same period, Yolo County citizens were also promoting efforts to tame the Sacramento River and to reclaim the land along its banks. The county authorized formation of reclamation districts whose property owners were assessed to pay the costs of constructing levees and canals. Two reclamation districts were created in Yolo County in 1870—R.D. No. 108, to reclaim 74,085.87 acres along the Sacramento River in northern Yolo and southern Colusa counties; and R.D. 150, to reclaim approximately 5,000 acres on Merritt Island (Clarksburg). Two other districts were formed in the county in the nineteenth century: R.D. 307 (Lisbon), formed in 1876 between Babel Slough and Merritt Island; and R.D. 537 (Lovdal), formed north of Washington in 1891. These four

The Yolo County Farm Bureau was organized on March 7, 1914. One of the day's speakers was B.H. Crocheron, the first director of the Agricultural Extension Service. He sent farm advisors from the University of California to counties where there were cooperating farm organizations, to disseminate technical information being developed through the Experiment Station. Local farm bureaus became an important part of the educational and social life in rural communities. Courtesy, Jane Morris Reiff

districts built levees around approximately 56,280 acres of productive farmland, but without a continuous levee along the Sacramento River, much of the eastern third of the county remained vulnerable to flooding until after 1900.

The first levees were built by hand—often by Chinese laborers using picks, shovels, and wheelbarrows. The first steam-powered clamshell dredge used in levee building in California was employed by R.D. 307 in 1879. That dredge had buckets that held approximately two cubic yards of mud, suspended on an 80-foot boom. With it, R.D. 307 built 14 miles of levees around its 6,000 acres, with levees ranging in height from six to 17 feet.

In 1907 a monster flood occurred. Water in the Sacramento River flowed at the rate of 600,000 cubic feet per second, or 100 times the normal flow. In January 1909 another flood occurred that washed out the railroad tracks between Sacramento, Davis, Woodland, and Marysville and isolated Knights Landing for five weeks. The outcry after that flood, combined with proposals by private developers to reclaim the American and Yolo basins, forced the legislature to approve the long-debated Sacramento Flood Control Plan.

The Flood Control Plan, signed into law in 1911, set up a partnership of federal, state, and local agencies to control the entire Sacra-

mento River. The idea was to increase the river's scouring power by channeling its waters between high levees and excavating the mouth of the river in Suisun Bay, and to lessen the danger of flooding by constructing several weirs in the levees that could be opened to release excess water harmlessly into bypasses.

One part of the plan was the Knights Landing Ridge Cut, designed to drain water from the Colusa Basin into the Yolo Basin. Construction of a 10-mile canal through the ridge, which was a naturally elevated strip of ground extending southwest from Knights Landing to higher land, began in 1914 and was completed in 1919. It cost $1 million and

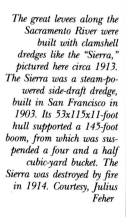

The great levees along the Sacramento River were built with clamshell dredges like the "Sierra," pictured here circa 1913. The Sierra was a steam-powered side-draft dredge, built in San Francisco in 1903. Its 53x115x11-foot hull supported a 145-foot boom, from which was suspended a four and a half cubic-yard bucket. The Sierra was destroyed by fire in 1914. Courtesy, Julius Feher

permitted the reclamation of 73,000 acres of the Colusa Basin.

Between 1870 and 1928, 21 reclamation districts were formed in the county, which built levees 15 to 30 feet high that protected nearly 200,000 acres of productive farmland at a total cost of over $11 million.

During the first two decades of the twentieth century, the patterns on the land along the river were dramatically altered as the swamps were drained and crops were planted in the newly reclaimed fields. During the same period developers found three areas in Yolo County particularly attractive: the old Fair Ranch north of Knights Landing, the farmland surrounding Washington, and the

rich bottomlands of Clarksburg and Merritt Island.

After the death of Charley Fair (son of Senator James Fair) in 1902, the Fair Ranch was sold in 1908 to the Sacramento River Farms Company—organized and financed by San Francisco and Eastern capitalists who planned to reclaim the land for farming. The company merged with the Yolo Land Company in 1916 and became the River Garden Farms Company of California. The 1940 *History of Yolo County* contained this description of River Garden Farms in the 1920s:

This enterprise, one of the largest of its kind in the

Above: "THE WATERS TRIUMPHANT ROLL OVER THE STREETS OF KNIGHTS LAND-ING," screamed the head-lines on January 25, 1909. Two major storms during the month of January caused breaks in the levees and isolated the town for five weeks. This picture, taken from the top floor of the schoolhouse looking north toward the Sacra-mento River, shows the river flowing freely through the streets, past the Meth-odist Church in the fore-ground and the United Brethren Church in the background. Courtesy, Nola Bohannon

Left: Tules once covered the swampy land near the Sa-cramento River. After the swamps were drained, the tules had to be broken up by heavy tractors and rollers before the ground could be plowed and planted. The ground had many sinkholes, some large enough to engulf a tractor. The man standing on the roof of the tractor was a lookout to warn the driver whenever a sinkhole was sighted. Courtesy, Friends of the Clarksburg Library

world, is a single ranch farmed entirely by one company and its equipment . . . Twenty-six hundred acres are set out to grain, barley, wheat, summer crops and rice. About twenty-one hundred acres are planted to orchard: pears, peaches and prunes. They also raise pure bred stock . . . The company has 295 buildings on one ranch, owns all its machinery, including pumping plants . . .

Reclamation rejuvenated the nearby town of Knights Landing. Its docks and warehouses were piled high with produce and its merchants supplied the needs of the farmers. The population doubled from 700 in 1920 to 1,400 in 1930.

The farmland surrounding Washington also attracted investors from San Francisco—the financiers of the Northern Electric Company (which was building an electric interurban railroad in the Sacramento Valley) who wanted land near downtown Sacramento for a railroad terminal. In 1907 they formed the West Sacramento Land Company to reclaim and develop 663.86 acres south of Washington.

The floods of 1907 and 1909 plus the costs of reclamation forced the company to reorganize. A new West Sacramento Company was incorporated in 1910, and within two years the company doubled its holdings to 11,202 acres, and began an ambitious program of land development.

The company began the job of reclaiming

its land across the river from Sacramento in 1911. Six years later, the job was virtually finished, and land was available for farms, homes, businesses, and industrial plants. Arthur F. Turner, the company's bookkeeper since 1913, became the company's manager in 1923 and spent the next 50 years promoting the development of West Sacramento.

The same San Francisco capitalists who had invested in West Sacramento began the work of reclaiming the area around Clarksburg. They incorporated the Netherlands Farms Company in 1912 and formed R.D. 999 the following year to reclaim 26,158 acres lying west of Elk Slough. (The founders envisaged a district that would resemble the Netherlands, with prosperous farms and a tidy little town protected from flooding by an intricate system of dikes.) The investors' financial difficulties in 1914 led them to pull out of this project, and a new company, the Holland Land Company, was formed in 1916.

Reclamation of the Holland District took about two years and involved 12 clamshell dredges. The company built 35 miles of levees, 150 miles of canals, one 175,000-gallon-a-minute pumping plant, and 18 subsidiary ones. The company also drained Big Lake and built 25 miles of roads, 100 bridges, telephone lines, and over 90 farm buildings.

The company began selling tracts in 1918. Company policy was to sell to a buyer not more than 3,000 acres, at a minimum of $250 an acre. Within 10 years, all but 1,700 acres of company land had been sold. Stockholders began receiving dividends in 1922, and continued to do so throughout the Depression. In 1942, with all its land in private hands and the maintenance of the reclamation system the responsibility of R.D. 999, the Holland Land Company was dissolved.

The company's plan of developing model farms and a model town succeeded to a great extent. The population of the Clarksburg area, which included Merritt Island and the Lisbon and Glide districts to the north, grew from 895 to 3,021 between 1910 and 1930, and Clarksburg became the social and commer-

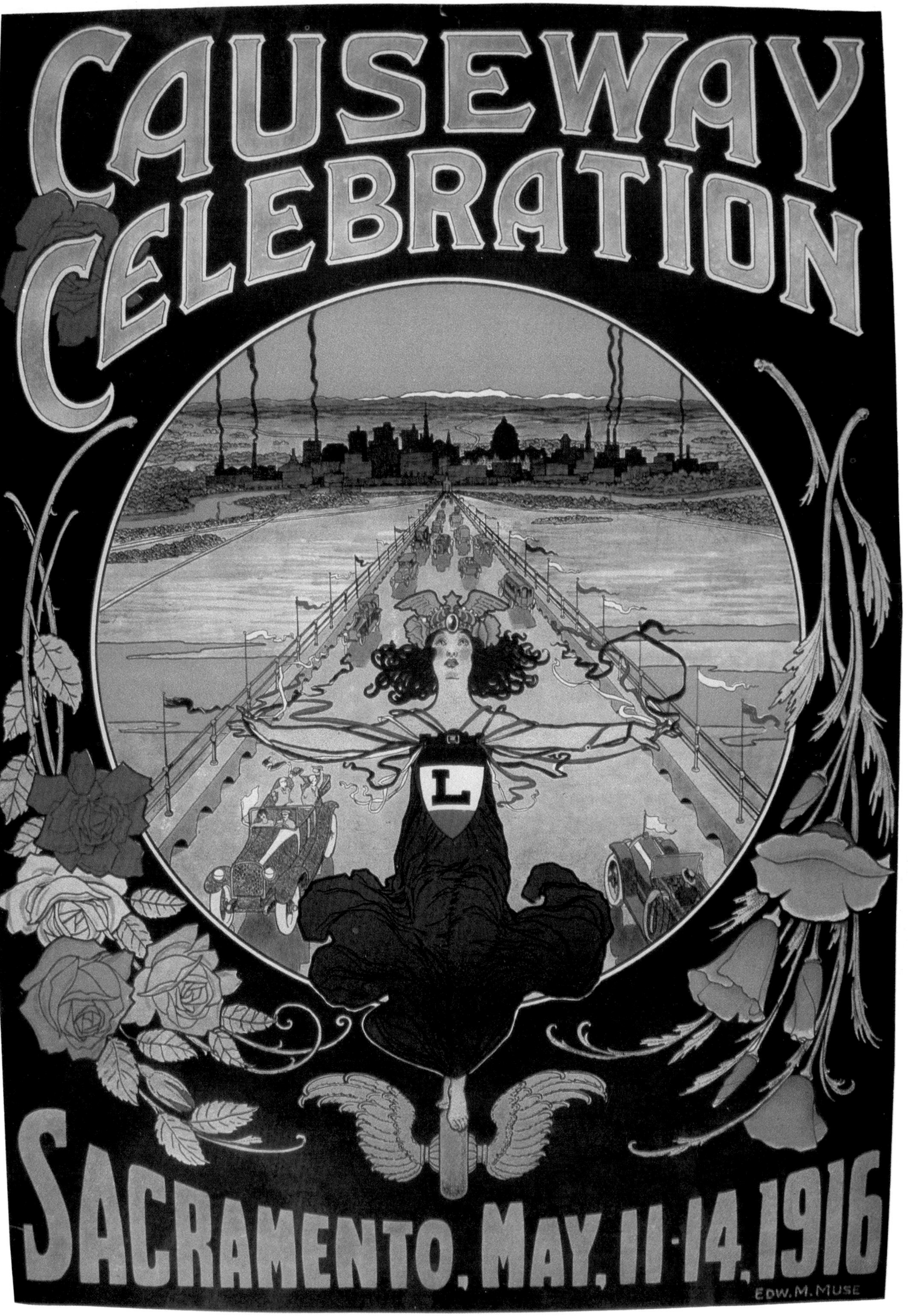
CAUSEWAY
CELEBRATION
L
SACRAMENTO, MAY, 11-14, 1916
EDW. M. MUSE

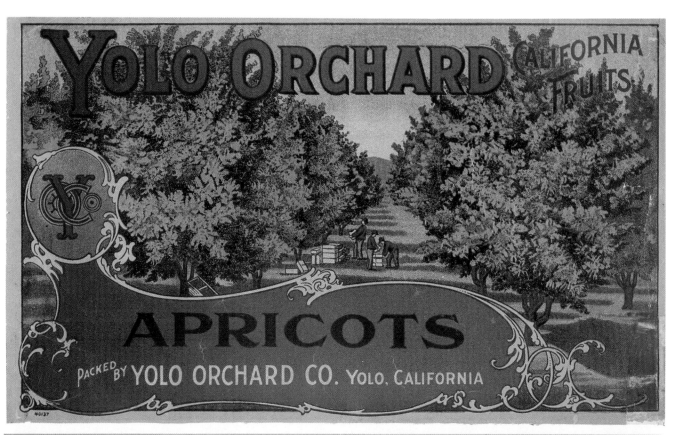

Left: This pastoral scene —a contrast between irrigated grainfields in the foreground and dry-farmed hills in the distance—was photographed in Oat Valley in 1967. It is a scene that would have looked the same 50 years ago, or in 1987, as the land use in this district has not changed significantly over the years. Courtesy, Earl A. Balch

Below, left: Before the vast reclamation projects of the twentieth century, about one-third of Yolo's land was covered with rank-growing reeds and grasses called "tules." The Patwin called the area yoloy, a land abounding in rushes, and that name was adopted for the county in 1850. Tules average 10 feet in height, and while they dominated the landscape, travel was difficult and land cultivation impossible. In the past 130 years, tules were cleared from almost all Yolo's land, and only a few stands remain. Courtesy, Shipley Walters

Facing page, top: This colorful label was designed by an unknown artist for the Yolo Orchard Company, a syndicated firm organized in 1890 that planted 400 acres near the town of Yolo with vines and fruit and nut trees. Courtesy, Jane Morris Reiff

Facing page, bottom: Extension of the Sacramento Northern Railroad in 1912 to farm centers west of the Sacramento River inspired the design for box labels of locally grown pears. Courtesy, Out of the West Publishing Co.

Above: This photo of cattle grazing on freshly cut grain stubble after the July harvest in 1986 duplicates a sequence of events that has occurred annually in the rolling hills of Hungry Hollow since German settlers first came to this region in the 1850s. Courtesy, Jack J. Potter

Right: Harbingers of spring, blossoms of the native redbud have annually attracted sightseers to Cache Creek and Putah Creek canyons since the advent of the automobile. Open touring cars, filled with sprays of rose-purple blossoms—like those seen in this 1975 photo taken in Putah Canyon—were sent to San Francisco on March 26, 1915, to add festive color to Yolo County Day at the Panama Pacific Exposition. Courtesy, Earl A. Balch

Left: Safflower is another crop grown for seed in Yolo County. Safflower seeds produce oil that is popular with nutritionists because it is high in poly-unsaturated linoleic acid. This oil is used in products such as salad oils and margarine. Safflower and wheat are highly competitive, and when wheat prices are high, less safflower is grown. Courtesy, Jack J. Potter

Right: An arched bicycle-pedestrian bridge over the Yolo-Solano County line adds grace and charm to the University Arboretum that borders Old Putah Creek. Started in 1936, the arboretum specializes in trees, shrubs, and flowers that grow well in the Sacramento Valley. Wooded paths along the water's edge make the arboretum a favorite retreat for those living in the Davis area. Courtesy, Richard F. Walters

Below, left: After a fire destroyed much of downtown Woodland in 1892, new buildings were constructed of brick. This three-story red sandstone building, which housed the Farmers and Merchants Bank, opened for business in January 1894. Two years later the Woodland Opera House was rebuilt next door. The building was torn down in 1970, and the lot was purchased by the Yolo County Historical Society for expansion of the opera house and an Opera House Plaza. Courtesy, Eleanor Emison

Far right: Mrak Hall, housing administrative offices on the UC Davis campus, looms five stories high over an enlarged basin along what is now the sealed-off original channel of Putah Creek. Built in 1966, the hall was named for Dr. Emil M. Mrak, UCD chancellor who guided the university's period of major growth from 1959 to 1969. Courtesy, Karen Froyland

Above: An aerial view of the Winters area, looking west in August 1986, shows the proximity of fruit orchards to the city and the clearings for eastward development. A golden patch of Faye Elberta peaches drying in the sun highlights the ranch of Gene and Marion Caselli, which has been sold for residential and commercial use. Courtesy, Stephen Caselli

Left: Overlapping trays of golden apricots lie in the California sunshine for a day of curing in this June 1986 photo, taken at the Gene Caselli fruit ranch just east of Winters. Courtesy, Stephen Caselli

Right: It was pumpkin time in 1982 when this colorful view of the Davis Farmers Market was taken. Started in 1976 when the "back to the farm movement" created public interest in farm-fresh fruits and vegetables, the market has developed into a year-round, biweekly attraction at the Davis Central Park and a profitable outlet for local farmers, craftpersons, and food vendors. Courtesy, Karen Froyland

Below, right: The Yolo County Historical Museum found a home in 1975 when the County of Yolo purchased the 12-room residence and 2.2-acre ranch headquarters of William B. and Mary I. Cook Gibson. Gibson, a successful farmer, made several additions to the home between 1857 and 1905. Now within the Woodland city limits, the residence and outbuildings have been restored for public use, with the assistance of many volunteer citizens. Courtesy, Jack J. Potter

cial center of an area some called "The Eden of California."

The massive reclamation and irrigation projects of the early twentieth century greatly increased the value of Yolo's farm property. According to reports of the California State Board of Agriculture, the number of acres under irrigation increased from 11,754 to 42,273. The value of farm property increased from $31,798,096 in 1910 to $66,248,770 in 1920.

In 1900 Yolo farmers were looking for more reliable sources of irrigation water. Farmers living near the Sacramento River had traditionally drawn water from the river through simple diversion dams and ditches. After 1918, when most of the large reclamation projects were in operation, they irrigated their fields in summer by reversing the pumps that had drained water from the land in winter.

Farmers who lived away from the river drilled wells on their property and pumped water to where it was needed. This source of water became economical after 1903 when electric power, originating from Folsom Dam on the American River, was extended to the Woodland area.

A third source of irrigation water for Yolo farmers was the series of ditches that diverted water from Cache Creek. Though these canals served most of the central portion of the county, their customers complained regularly about tardy and inadequate deliveries of water.

In 1903 a group of Yolo County landowners and investors, led by Joseph Craig, a wealthy Woodland lawyer, organized the Yolo County Consolidated Water Company which in turn bought the Adams, Capay, and Woodland canal companies and acquired the right to build dams to impound the waters of Clear Lake and Cache Creek "for use, distribution and power purposes."

Craig and his partners had ambitious plans. Between 1904 and 1908, after groups of farmers formed ditch companies and subscribed the necessary funds, the company built canals that brought water from Cache Creek to the Madison, Winters, and Davis areas. As a result another 100,000 acres in Yolo and Solano counties were brought under irrigation.

Two years later the company purchased 2,400 acres of land at the lower end of Clear Lake where it planned to build a dam and power plant. Although those plans fell through, the company did extend irrigation ditches north to Blacks and south to Dixon in Solano County. The company was bought out by the Yolo Water and Power Company, incorporated in 1912 by a group of Oakland and San Francisco investors.

This company built a dam five miles below the outlet of Clear Lake, and an impounding dam on Cache Creek, two miles upstream from Capay. Between 1912 and 1917 the company spent $500,000 in Yolo County on dams, canals, and distribution gates, and in 1916 it delivered 69,000 acre-feet of water to its 600 customers.

Changes resulted from the increased use of irrigation and new market demands. With the improvement of irrigation facilities, more and more farmers began to grow rice. Acreage in rice increased from 1,500 acres in 1915 to 20,000 acres in 1921.

Between 1910 and 1921 the types of orchard trees grown changed noticeably. Nut trees increased from 184,000 to 337,379 while fruit trees dropped from 521,135 to 373,437. Eucalyptus, first planted as a lumber crop in 1909 near Dunnigan, proved to be a commercial failure.

Sugar beets were very promising in 1910 when farmers planted 5,714 acres, valued at $200,000. By 1920, however, there were only 120 acres of this crop, because a virus disease killed off nearly all the beets.

Like the farmers, railroadmen continued to expand operations in Yolo County in the early 1900s.

The Sacramento-Woodland Railroad, a Northern Electric subsidiary, was completed in 1912. This electric interurban line extended 17.93 miles from Sacramento to Woodland. The company also built a bridge across the Sacramento River at M Street. After

Preparations for an excursion of the Winters Driving Club were being made when this photo was taken in 1909 along the north side of East Main Street. Seated in the first car, in front of their home, are David O. Judy and his daughter Grace. Judy's son Roe and Miss McSall are in the second vehicle. Judy, owner of the local livery stable, and his stepson Charles Elliot later went into the automobile and bus business themselves. Courtesy, Yolo County Historical Museum

several years of financial difficulties, the railroad was sold in 1918 to the Sacramento Northern Railroad which continued to operate it until 1940.

Another electric interurban line built through Yolo County was the Oakland, Antioch and Eastern Railroad. This line ran from Oakland to West Sacramento and Sacramento.

In 1913 the West Sacramento Company offered electric streetcar service between downtown Sacramento and West Sacramento. The streetcar operated until 1925 when it was abandoned as too costly.

The West Sacramento Company also organized the West Side Railroad in 1911 to haul freight along the west side of the Sacramento River to Rio Vista. Unfortunately the company ran out of money after 600 feet of track were laid, but it ran freight through West Sacramento on OA&E lines. In 1925 a branch line opened south to Clarksburg.

A new form of transportation—the bicycle—started a national Good Roads Movement. The bicycle rage of the 1890s led to the formation of bicycle clubs whose members lobbied for better roads and separate "wheelways."

Cycling clubs formed at Davis and Woodland in the mid-1890s. On May 11, 1894, the *Yolo Weekly Mail* of Woodland reported:

About twenty-five members of the Bicycle Club, ladies and gentlemen, made their appearance on our streets last evening on their favorite steeds, and presented a very handsome appearance. They executed some very pretty maneuvers on Main street, and their riding was both graceful and attractive . . . The young ladies especially enjoy the outing, and some of them are expert riders . . .

Women riders were not so well received at Davis in 1895, when it was reported that "nine lone and unprotected bloomer girls from Sacramento shocked the staid morals of our town Saturday and Sunday."

With the introduction of the automobile, drives in the country soon became a favorite

Left: The people of Winters chose to represent their area in the "Grand Decorated Causeway Floral Parade" of May 13, 1916, with a float made of dried fruit representing their new high school building. A crowd of 100,000 watched the three-mile parade in Sacramento that celebrated the opening of the first year-round road across the Yolo Basin. Courtesy, Warren A. Westgate

Below: The Yolo Causeway was a vital link in the California state highway system for it was the first all-year, all-weather bridge across the Yolo Basin between Sacramento and Davis. When it was completed in 1916—3.1 miles long, 20 feet high, and 21 feet wide—it was the longest concrete highway trestle in the world. Courtesy, Carroll Cross

pastime. The County of Yolo oiled the surface of the most frequently used roads and replaced dozens of old wooden bridges with reinforced concrete structures.

Increased automobile traffic during this period also led the State of California to improve its roadways. In 1911 the state began building a state highway west from Sacramento to San Francisco. The paved road led from the M Street Bridge to the eastern edge of the Yolo Basin, across the Yolo Bypass on an elevated two-lane causeway, and west to Davis and Dixon.

The Yolo Causeway, which was 3.1 miles long and cost $400,000 to build, was completed in 1916. Thousands celebrated the opening of the causeway and the first all-year, all-weather road across the tules.

Construction of a north-south state highway got underway in 1914, with a Yolo-Solano bridge over Putah Creek and a road north via CR 98 to Brown's Corner west of Woodland. From there it crossed Cache Creek at the town of Yolo, and continued north to Zamora and Dunnigan.

Yolo County began to modernize its highway system in 1917. By 1919 there were 111 miles of paved roads in the county. That same year county voters approved a $990,000 bond issue for the construction and improvement of roads and bridges in the county. Funds for planting shade trees along county roads were also allocated, a beautification effort that was assisted by women's improvement clubs, Boy Scouts, the American Legion, and other service organizations.

Woodland nurse Ella Childers Doster (standing, fourth from right) commanded an ambulance corps in World War I. She served as a Red Cross nurse in France before the U.S. entered the war, and received a medal for bravery at Verdun in 1916. In 1917 she received a commission in the U.S. army and served in France until the Armistice. Courtesy, Don Urain

6

HARD TIMES AND GOOD TIMES

1916-1946

On March 9, 1916, the civil war in Mexico spilled over into the United States when rebel leader Pancho Villa raided Columbus, New Mexico, and killed 17 Americans. Local units of the National Guard were mobilized to defend the U.S. border, and Woodland's Company F was ordered to join the First Brigade, Second California Infantry, in Nogales, Arizona.

On June 27, 1916, 74 men from Woodland, uniformed and armed, left by train for the border town. Six months later they returned home, well-trained but untested in battle.

When the United States entered World War I in 1917, men immediately began volunteering for service. Nineteen young men from Broderick joined the navy and sailed off together on the USS *Huntington*. Women served too. Verna Fox and Ida Nicals of Woodland enlisted in the navy as Yeomanettes, and Ella Childers Doster served overseas as a nurse. Over 900 Yoloans served in World War I; 32 never returned.

Even though most farmers were draft-exempt, many of them left their farms to serve in the armed forces or work in war-related industries. Hiring farmworkers became a critical problem in Yolo County, especially during harvest time. Women and children joined those men who remained, and participated in all phases of farming. Leila Hecke became manager of her father's apricot shed near Woodland soon after

her graduation from high school in 1918.

Women also took the place of men in business and other public sectors. The Woodland City Board of Trustees gained its first woman member with the appointment of Lydia Lawhead in 1915.

During the war 14 Liberty Leagues were organized in the county. League members succeeded in getting 13,000 subscribers for war bonds and stamps from a county with a population of 13,926, and raised $4,539,900.

All over the United States, chapters of the American Red Cross, inactive since the Spanish-American War, were being organized. A Red Cross chapter was formally organized in May 1917 in Woodland. By the following February, there were 4,903

members in 11 branch chapters, one high school auxiliary, and the Glenwood chapter, organized by the black women of the county. With the help of the Red Cross, Yolo farmers produced crops worth $30 million and were commended by President Woodrow Wilson.

When the Spanish influenza epidemic hit Yolo County in 1918, local ordinances were passed that prohibited all public gatherings. In Woodland the Byrns Hotel was made an emergency hospital. The Woodland Home Guard sent members to help there, as did the Red Cross. The Red Cross also offered free vaccination against the flu.

Then on November 11, 1918, the Armistice was signed and the war was over. "TOWN GOES WILD WHEN TRUCE COMES," cried the *Mail* of Woodland that day. An impromptu parade of a thousand people, led by the Home Guard, marched through the streets of Woodland at midnight for an hour, and plans were quickly made for a County Jubilee the next evening.

Yolo County emerged prosperous from the war, principally due to increased agricultural production to meet the demand for food

during the war and the foreign relief efforts that began when the war ended. The Esparto *Exponent* of December 26, 1919, reported that the county's bank roll had increased $2 million that year to $10 million. "This shows an increased per capital wealth of $736.72 for every man, woman and child of the 13,926 population."

During that boom year of 1919, Yolo County hosted a picnic for 15,000 people at Nelson's Grove, a picturesque grove of native oak trees north of Woodland. It was sponsored by the Fourteen Counties Protective Association to give thanks for the prosperity enjoyed in the Sacramento and San Joaquin valleys. The gala celebration on Saturday, June 21, lasted from morning until midnight.

No liquor was served at the picnic, for

Left: Sarah Laugenour Huston was an intelligent and energetic Woodland matron who was affectionately known as "Aunt Sally." She was an active member of the WCTU from its organization in Woodland in 1883 until her death in 1926, and for 35 years she edited and published the Home Alliance, *a weekly newspaper which promoted temperance and women's suffrage. Courtesy, Yolo County Historical Society*

Below, left: This Filipino laborer is packing asparagus on the J.W. Hollenbeck Ranch, on land reclaimed by the Holland Land Company near Clarksburg. Many Filipinos were employed in the Clarksburg area during the 1920s and 1930s, in the cultivation, cutting, and packing of the delicate asparagus. This photograph was taken in June 1926 when asparagus production in the area was at its peak. After the 1930s, asparagus was grown principally in San Joaquin County and near Woodland. Courtesy, Friends of the Clarksburg Library

Prohibition had gone into effect on January 29, 1919. Yolo County, with its many barley, hop, and grape growers, had voted against the Eighteenth Amendment in 1918, despite vigorous efforts by temperance advocates within the county.

Woman's Christian Temperance Union chapters had been organized in 1883 in Woodland and Cacheville, and others soon followed in Davis, Winters, Knights Landing, Madison, Guinda, Brooks, and Rumsey. The women worked not only against "demon rum," but for civic improvements and suffrage.

In 1911 women in California won the right to vote in state and local elections, and 400 Woodland women immediately registered. When the city held an election in December to decide whether saloons should be closed or not, saloon supporters lost by 318 votes.

Although Prohibition forced the closure of saloons, breweries, and wineries, it did not stop the consumption or production of alcohol. Wine, beer, and whiskey were manufactured in the quiet neighborhoods of Broderick (which also had speakeasies), Knights Landing, Blacks, Dunnigan, Woodland, and in the Capay Valley. The passage of the Twenty-first Amendment repealing

Prohibition in 1933 did not end bootlegging, and raids on illicit liquor sellers continued.

By the mid-twenties the merchants and farmers of Yolo County were recovering from a postwar slump. On August 23, 1926, the Woodland *Democrat* published a promotional booklet, *Yolo County in Word and Picture*, which announced proudly that "Anything that Grows Anywhere, Grows Everywhere in Yolo County."

The county gained worldwide fame for its purebred livestock. In 1920 there were 154,065 head of cattle, horses, mules, asses and burros, swine, sheep, and goats raised in Yolo County. That year Gordon H. True, professor at the College of Agriculture, counted 108 herds and flocks of purebred livestock within 25 miles of the Davis campus.

Yolo stockmen entered their animals in the International Livestock Exposition at Chicago and won prizes each year, including four purple grand championship ribbons in 1925 alone. The name "Purple Circle" was coined to describe the area around Davis in which so many grand champions were produced, and in March 1929 Yolo stockmen formed an organization with that same name. They also advertised their livestock with the Purple Circle emblem.

The livestock industry in California faced the worst crisis in its history in February 1924, when the dreaded hoof-and-mouth disease was discovered in West Berkeley. Within days of the discovery, George H. Hecke, the successful Woodland orchardist who was appointed the first director of the California Department of Agriculture in 1919, ordered a quarantine in 12 counties around the Bay Area. Arizona and Oregon slapped an embargo on all farm products from California, and within three months the state's economy dropped 18 percent. Hecke gave orders to slaughter all infected and exposed animals, dispose of the carcasses in trenches, and clean and disinfect the surrounding area. Hecke personally guaranteed a loan of $250,000 to begin the eradication program.

Eradicating the disease from California took two years and cost $4,350,008. Nearly

An epidemic of hoof-and-mouth disease almost wiped out livestock production in Northern California in 1924. To stop the epidemic, all infected animals were shot, buried in trenches, and the surrounding area was disinfected. Courtesy, River Garden Farms Collection, Yolo County Archives

110,000 farm animals and 22,214 wild deer were killed, including the famous milk cow, Tilly Alcartra. Hecke's daughter, Leila Hecke Hardy, commented that when Tilly had to be shot, "Dad was criticized around here for that more than for anything else I ever knew."

Between the two wars, Yolo County remained primarily rural. There were three incorporated cities—Davis, Winters, and Woodland (which was the largest with a population of 7,000). With the exception of Broderick, Bryte, and West Sacramento which lay directly across the river from downtown Sacramento, the other unincorporated communities were small social and supply centers for nearby farms.

In 1926 there were 41 school districts in Yolo County. Between 1917 and 1930, Yoloans built 14 new school buildings in the county—nine elementary schools and five high school buildings. They also built 11 new church buildings during this period.

The county's two hospitals were both located in Woodland—Yolo County Hospital, which dated from 1869; and Woodland Clinic Hospital, established in 1911. People in outlying communities went to their local schoolhouse for health services provided by

the County Health Department. Dr. Ruth Risdon Storer, a pediatrician who lived in Davis, helped establish well-baby clinics throughout the county. She regularly visited the clinics herself until she turned 80.

Communication was surprisingly rapid during this period. Telephones were becoming common and mail was delivered daily, even in the country. There were also eight newspapers: in Woodland, the *Mail*,

Above: The Church of the Holy Myrrh-bearing Women, located in Bryte, was built by a group of approximately 25 Russian Orthodox families. It was built by the men in their spare time, using plans designed by 16-year-old Nicholas Koshell, one of the neighborhood high school students. Money for construction was raised by the Russian women. The church was consecrated on May 15, 1927. Courtesy, Louisa Roma Vessell

Left: Tilly Alcartra, prize-winning Holstein cow owned by A.W. Morris & Sons, Woodland, is shown at a meeting of the San Francisco Ad Club in the Palace Hotel in 1920. That year an Ohio farm magazine writer commented, "If you should put all of the milk products produced last year by Tilly Alcartra, the world's champion cow, in 10-gallon cans and stack them pyramid fashion, the peak would be as high as an eight-story building." Courtesy, C.L. Eddy & Sons Collection, Yolo County Archives

Democrat, and *Home Alliance*; in Davis, the *Enterprise* and the *California Aggie* on the college campus; in Winters, the *Express*; in Esparto, the *Exponent*; and in Broderick, the *Independent-Leader*.

Two communities were developed in the county during this period—Bryte and West Sacramento. Bryte was named for George Bryte, Sr., son of the pioneer dairyman Mike Bryte. In 1920 Bryte had about 200 homes, occupied mainly by immigrant families of workers in the railyards of Sacramento. The town resembled a European village, with

small houses surrounded by vegetable gardens. One regularly heard Italian, Portuguese, and Russian spoken on the streets.

West Sacramento developed slowly, with fewer than 200 homes sold by 1920. Many of the householders commuted to jobs in Sacramento; the rest farmed or worked in local businesses. South of town was "the district," R.D. 900, where sugar beets, rice, tomatoes, and vegetables were grown.

During the twenties the west bank of the Sacramento River, with its riverboats and peaceful settings, attracted the motion picture industry. The river scenes in such films as *Tom Sawyer, Show Boat,* and *Steamboat 'Round the Bend* were filmed there. Knights Landing and Broderick were particularly popular as movie locations.

The boom years of the twenties came to an abrupt end in 1929 with the crash of the American stock market. Yolo County's agriculture, businesses, and labor were thoroughly disrupted during the Great Depression.

By 1930 agricultural prices on the world market had dropped drastically from their 1920 levels. Wheat was down from $2.50 to $1. Fruit prices dropped too: peaches went from $4.15 to $1.82; apricots from $3.85 to $2.

Frosts in 1929, 1930, and 1932 decimated

the orchards of western Yolo County, and a severe drought in 1931 compounded the damage. In 1931 only 250 carloads of fruit were shipped from Winters, compared to 2,000 carloads in 1919. Farmers curtailed all but necessary spending and drew more money out of the bank. Luckily, the banks of Yolo County were generally sound, and only two banks failed. In 1933 the Bank of Esparto and the Davis and Woodland branches of the Bank of Yolo closed permanently, although in time all depositors were repaid. Still, some families lost their farms through bank foreclosure or nonpayment of taxes.

In 1932, when the county's population was 23,644, there were about 2,100 unemployed. Farm laborers from the Philippines and Mexico shared the fate of local farmworkers whose jobs were cut back or eliminated during the thirties. Their ranks were swelled by migrant laborers from Mexico and the Dust Bowl regions who came looking for seasonal work.

"Hobo villages" popped up along the Sacramento River in Broderick and Knights Landing, and on the outskirts of many interior towns. In Winters, where 300 migrant men, women, and children were camped south of Putah Creek, union members came in and threatened to stage a hunger march on June 2, 1932. Local townspeople and county officials defused a potentially violent situation by providing food and relief supplies for the hungry. The three organizers of the march were tried and found guilty of promoting a disturbance. Legitimate farm labor organizers had better luck in the summer of 1936, when American Federation of Labor locals were formed throughout the Sacramento Valley, including one in Knights Landing.

The County of Yolo did the best it could

Above: During the early 1930s thousands of seasonal workers poured into the Sacramento Valley, camping where they could. In January 1935 the Federal Resettlement Administration provided funds to establish sanitary camps for harvest workers. Gonzales' camp for sugar beet workers was located north of Woodland. Courtesy, Yolo County Archives

Left: Sugar beets were a major farm crop in Yolo County in the 1930s. Here trucks on the levee near Clarksburg await their turn to unload their beets to a barge to be shipped out for processing. Beets were refined locally after Amalgamated Sugar Company built a sugar refinery in Clarksburg in 1934. Courtesy, Friends of the Clarksburg Library

depleted by the 1931 drought.

The *Daily Democrat* of March 23, 1936, reported that $64,550 was spent on Works Progress Administration (WPA) projects in Yolo County during the previous six months. Half the money was spent on roads, sidewalks, curbs, and gutters; the other half on construction and landscaping of public buildings and schools.

Things were improving in the private sector also. In January 1936 the California Turkey Growers' Association announced the opening of a precooling and packing plant in Knights Landing. Amalgamated Sugar Company built a mill in Clarksburg in 1934,

Above: A new concrete highway bridge was constructed across the Sacramento River at Knights Landing in 1933. Courtesy, Yolo County Archives

Right: The $2.5-million Spreckels Sugar Plant near Woodland opened on July 1, 1937, with a three-day celebration. An estimated 30,000 people visited the factory during the opening weekend, which featured Yolo County's first Sugar Queen contest. The contest is still held annually in July, and the queen is crowned at the county fair in August. The plant, still in operation, handles 3,600 tons of sugar beets a day during harvest time. Courtesy, Yolo County Archives

during the Depression. It paid unemployed workers $1 a day to work on the roads, and also reduced salaries of county department heads and teachers.

In 1929 the county joined with Sutter County and the State of California to build a highway from Woodland through Knights Landing to Yuba City. A new concrete bascule bridge over the Sacramento River at Knights Landing was opened on December 1, 1933, and a crowd of 1,500 people gathered for the day-long celebration.

By 1936 there were signs of recovery within the county as President Roosevelt's New Deal started to take effect. Rural electrification projects made electrical milking machines feasible. Also important were irrigation projects. A 10-foot percolation dam was built in 1936 on Putah Creek at Winters that improved the area's water table that had been

and Spreckels Sugar Company completed its refinery north of Woodland in 1937. The following year Yolo was the leading sugar beet county in the United States, with 36,000 acres planted to beets.

In 1936 the Capay Almond Growers' Association signed a contract to sell its crop for prices ranging from 17 to 26.15 cents, double the previous year's price. Also in 1936, the price of barley rose 100 percent over the previous year's, to $1.40 per hundred pounds. The newspapers of 1937 told of remodeling and reopenings of stores, rising prices, and rising hopes. The Davis *Enterprise* of February 5, 1937, commented, "The unsightly wooden awnings, a relic of the 'horse and buggy days,' have been torn down, thus taking a forward step in the improvement of the business district."

The business district of Knights Landing

was dramatically remodeled on September 17, 1938, by a fire that started on Front Street. Within hours Front Street was destroyed. After the fire, new businesses were built along Locust Street, facing the highway that passed through Knights Landing.

Most of Yolo County had already recovered from the Depression when the Japanese bombed Pearl Harbor on December 7, 1941, and the United States was plunged into global war.

Members of the Woodland National Guard were among the first to see active service in the war. The same day war was declared, Woodland's Headquarters Company was sent to San Diego for assignment to the army's Seventh Infantry Division. The unit served in the Aleutians, Marshall Islands, Philippines, and in Okinawa. After the war, it was sent to Korea to disarm and repatriate Japanese prisoners of war.

Many Yoloans, male and female, served in the armed forces. Every community in Yolo County had service flags, with blue stars for service personnel and gold stars to commemorate those killed in action. By the end of the war, there were 142 gold stars on the county flag.

After the Japanese attack on Hawaii, bombing, invasion, or sabotage by the Japanese was considered a real threat on the West Coast. People began distrusting their Japanese neighbors, even in places like Clarksburg and Winters where Japanese families had lived and worked for 50 years. By January 1942 Japanese schools in Clarksburg, Bryte, and Winters, which served as community centers, were ordered closed. On February 16, the City of Winters demanded that all Japanese be removed from the community.

Three days later President Roosevelt issued Executive Order 9066 which gave the Western Defense Command authority over Japanese living in the U.S. On March 27 the command ordered all Japanese, whether alien or U.S. born, interned in camps for the duration of the war. The Japanese were ordered to liquidate their property within seven days. Many of those in Yolo County, primarily farmers, leased their land, sold their farm equipment at a loss, and left their belongings with friends.

Over 1,000 Japanese were evacuated from

The Woodland Chapter of the Red Cross sponsored a canteen on Main Street for the servicemen from nearby air force, army, and navy bases to use during their stay in Woodland during World War II. The Red Cross used the hall of Yolo Post No. 77, American Legion, for the weekly servicemen's dance. Girls from Yolo County volunteered as hostesses. Courtesy, Yolo Post No. 77, American Legion, Woodland

Members of the Woodland National Guard served with the 184th Infantry Regiment, U.S. army, from 1941-1946. Here the war-weary soldiers manage smiles on Christmas Day, 1944, at Ormac, Leyte, Philippine Islands. Left to right in the back row are J. Holland, Hughes, Leggins, and Maccelli; front row: Dyer, Willis, M. Holland, Cook, Lattimer, Urain, Bobb, and Chandler. Courtesy, Don Urain

Yolo County between May and June. They were imprisoned at a camp in Tule Lake, California, until September 7, 1945. Very few returned to their former homes. Those who did found few of the belongings they had left behind.

Immediately after war was declared, county supervisors appointed a Civil Defense Board to coordinate all wartime defense activities—agricultural production, medical care, rationing, blackouts, plane spotting, and the like. Yolo County Agricultural Commissioner Charles H. Hardy was made chairman, assisted by the sheriff, farm advisor, and a number of elected and appointed officials.

Yolo citizens quickly adjusted to wartime conditions. They planted Victory Gardens, bought savings bonds, donated blood, rolled bandages, gathered scrap metal, blackened their windows at night, conducted air raid drills, and coped with ration stamps for sugar, meat, shoes, gasoline, and tires.

At the College of Agriculture at Davis, regular classes were suspended in February 1943 when the campus was turned over to the

U.S. army as a training center for the Army Signal Corps. The sounds of bugles, army vehicles, and 2,000 marching men were heard regularly until October 1945 when the campus reverted to the university. During this time many Davis families shared their homes with the families of the trainees.

Yolo County farmers did their bit for Uncle Sam by increasing production to an all-time high. Despite price freezes, farm income more than doubled during the war.

Hiring farmworkers became difficult as many able-bodied men and women left for the armed forces or war-related industries. Neighbors—men, women, and children—turned out to help at harvest time. High schools were closed during the tomato harvest so that students and teachers could pick the ripe fruit. Navajo Indians were bussed in from reservations in Arizona and New Mexico, and Mexican workers were actively recruited.

When the war ended in 1945, church bells rang all over Yolo County, and people thronged the streets, rejoicing at the end of a tumultuous era.

White-collar "gandy dancers" from Davis joined Southern Pacific section crews on weekends to help the war effort on the home front. Pictured in 1942 are some of the 100 Davis businessmen, high school and college students, and university professors who put in eight-and-a-half-hour days for $6.40 resetting rails and transferring freight shipments. Local Southern Pacific Agent A.G. Brinley's idea of using community workers to offset critical labor shortages was so successful that the "Davis Idea" was implemented throughout the Southern Pacific system, bringing national recognition in Time *magazine to this small Yolo County city. Courtesy, John W. Brinley*

*The city of West Sacramento, which incorporated on January 1, 1987, is located directly across the Sacramento River from
downtown Sacramento. This photograph shows the patterns on the land: the winding Sacramento River (right), the
right-angle curve of the Deep Water Channel (left) and turning basin of the Sacramento-Yolo Port (center), the concrete
ribbons of freeways (upper center), the plaids of city streets, and the patchwork of agricultural fields.
Courtesy, Cartwright Aerial Surveys, Inc.*

7

RADIATING PATTERNS

1946-1987

In the post-World War II era, as labor costs rose and the pool of farmworkers decreased, California farmers looked to mechanization to solve their problems. The University of California, through agricultural research and technology, revolutionized not only the way many crops were planted, irrigated, cultivated, harvested, and transported, but also the form and varieties of the crops themselves. University scientists also developed new fertilizers, chemicals for insect and weed control, and improved feed mixes for livestock.

University scientists experimented with mechanization years before the war. The profits of Yolo rice farmers were increased by the development, beginning in 1929, of machinery that reduced the need for human labor and improved the quantity and quality of marketable rice. Yolo's wheat, corn, and alfalfa crops also were aided by university-developed machines, as were Yolo orchardists. Tree-knockers were developed for almond and walnut trees and wire trellises and vibrators for grapevines. Even prunes were mechanically harvested. Three laborers, using a tree-shaker and two portable catching frames, could pick 60 prune trees per hour.

John B. Powers of the Agricultural Experiment Station at UC Davis perfected a machine in 1942 that topped and loaded sugar beets in the field. That same year the Marbeet Harvester was invented. Then Lysle D. Leach, a plant pathologist at UC Davis, worked with Roy Bainer of

ented jointly by the University of California and the manufacturer, Ernest Blackwelder of Rio Vista—the first time the university had given permission to use "UC" in the name of a commercial product. Another harvester, with a different shaking mechanism, was developed by Robert Button on his ranch near Winters.

Widespread use of the tomato harvester began with the termination of the Bracero Program in 1964. Under this program, which began during World War II, the U.S. Department of Agriculture recruited, contracted with, transported, and fed much-needed Mexican farmworkers. When the program

Above: Rice became a major Yolo crop during World War I when wartime increased production and prices. After the war airplanes were used in seeding and cultivating rice. Water-soaked rice kernels were dropped into flooded rice checks where they sprouted quickly. Later insect and animal pests were controlled by aerial spraying. In the fall rice was harvested by huge mechanical harvesters, dried in rice driers, and shipped in bulk to domestic and foreign markets. Courtesy, California State Library

Above, right: This mechanical tomato harvester is shown moving through a field of ripe tomatoes on the Heringer Bros. farm near Clarksburg. The machine cuts and conveys the tomatoes into bulk bins for sorting and loading into gondolas to be trucked to the cannery. Human labor required for harvesting tomatoes was cut 80 percent by the use of the mechanical harvester. Courtesy, Special Collections, UCD Library

the Department of Agricultural Engineering to develop a sugar beet seed that increased yield and reduced the need for hand thinning in the field. By 1958 100 percent of the sugar beet crop in the county was harvested by machine.

The UC Tomato Harvester was the result of a unique combination of scientific talents on the Davis campus. The agricultural engineer, Coby Lorenzen, designed a machine that could cut tomatoes and load them into gondolas in the field. The vegetable crop specialist, Jack Hanna, developed a tomato that had specific qualities required by mechanical harvesting. The machine was pat-

ended in 1964, the resulting shortage of labor forced growers to mechanize. By 1975 100 percent of the tomato harvesting was done by machine.

In 1961, just as mechanical harvesting of tomatoes was beginning, Hunt-Wesson Company built a plant northeast of Davis, similar to Contadina's tomato-processing plant in Woodland, built in 1942. Both plants continue to operate.

Although Yolo farmers eased some of their burden through mechanization, flood control and irrigation development were still problems in the 1950s along Cache and Putah creeks. The $46-million Yolo-Solano Recla-

The Bracero Program supplied legal Mexican laborers for work on California farms between 1942 and 1964. Many of these farmworkers were employed in Yolo County's tomato fields, where they planted, cultivated, and harvested the county's most valuable crop. Mexican families lived temporarily in labor camps, and children often accompanied their parents all day in the hot fields. Photo by Margery Mann. Courtesy, Yolo County Historical Museum

mation Development on Putah Creek was completed in 1957, which included construction of Monticello Dam and creation of a lake 25 miles long in the Berryessa Valley of Napa County. Although Yoloans opted not to receive one half of the irrigation water to which they were entitled from this project, the Lake Berryessa Reservoir quickly became a popular recreational area.

The Yolo County Flood Control and Water Conservation District, created by the state legislature in 1957, succeeded in getting a $4.4-million bond issue passed in 1972 to build a 225-foot dam on the North Fork of Cache Creek, inundating Indian Valley. The dam created the 300,000-acre-foot-capacity Indian Valley Reservoir to supply water for irrigation and recreation. The entire project ultimately cost $10 million and was completed in 1976.

In 1967 the district also acquired the Clear Lake Water Company. With water from Clear Lake and Indian Valley, the district in 1987 irrigated 55,000 acres of farmland through 190 miles of canals and operated two hydroelectric plants.

Some basic water problems that have been the source of protracted litigation over the years still plagued landowners in Yolo and Lake counties in the 1980s—flood damage, erosion control, groundwater recharge, gravel mining, and the amount of water that should or should not be taken out of Clear Lake at various seasons of the year. Solutions to these problems were still being studied by federal, state, and county agencies.

Farming in Yolo County has become a complex business. Agricultural technology is more complicated, so specialized education and training are required for today's farmers.

Governmental price supports require sophisticated accounting by recipients, and more and more farms now use computers and business management practices.

Statistics show that in 1979, 21 crops earned more than $1 million, led by tomatoes which brought in a whopping $91.9 million that year. Other leading crops were the traditional ones—wheat, rice, corn, sugar beets, nuts, and livestock—along with some new ones—safflower, grain sorghum, sunflowers, kiwi fruit, and pistachios. Statistics also show that more acres were farmed (510,000 in 1950, 566,000 in 1979), but there were fewer farms (1,263 in 1950, 927 in 1979), and farm income was up dramatically ($56,460,000 in 1954, $240,399,260 in 1979).

Yolo's population began to grow rapidly immediately after World War II, as did the population of the state. Situated along the major travel routes between San Francisco, Sacramento, and points north and east, Yolo attracted new residents who liked its climate, rural atmosphere, and educational institutions. By 1950 its population had grown in 10 years from 27,243 to 40,640. By 1980 the population was 113,374. Its people in 1979 were white (77 percent), Mexican-American (11 percent), black (1.2 percent), Japanese (1.1 percent), Chinese (.8 percent), Filipino, Punjabi, Pakistani, Vietnamese, and Cambodian.

Yolo County began to plan for growth before World War II. In the late 1930s West Sacramento residents urged the County of Yolo to protect their property from haphazard community development. The county prepared a master plan for East Yolo, with a zoning ordinance to enforce it. In 1942 master plans and zoning ordinances were approved for the cities of Woodland and Davis and the towns of Clarksburg, Knights Landing, and Esparto. The city of Winters had a planning commission and zoning ordinance by 1947.

When the postwar construction boom began in 1946, the county began requiring building permits and hired its first full-time building inspector. The county adopted its first building code in 1956, and hired its first professional planning director, Herbert G. Hotchner, in 1957. Hotchner's task was to

The pattern of agricultural development in the upper Capay Valley has changed very little since this aerial photo was taken in 1964 from a point near Brooks, looking northwest. Today there are more walnut orchards than plantings of almonds and fruit trees. But grain is still grown, the central road (SH 16) that opened to the Clear Lake area in 1934 still traces the route of the railroad tracks that were removed the same year, and Cache Creek continues to carve its course against the Capay Ridge on the right. Courtesy, Department of the Interior, Bureau of Reclamation

plan for the county and its three cities. He was backed by the farm bureau, which feared Yolo County's farms and orchards would soon be encroached upon by freeways and subdivisions.

In 1965 the legislature passed the Williamson Act. Under this act, farmers were encouraged to have their land zoned "Agricultural Preserve," thereby assuring that their land would be assessed at low agricultural rates for 10 years. By 1987, 72.61 percent of all Yolo County's land was in agricultural preserve.

Throughout the sixties, seventies, and eighties various elements of the county's master plan, as well as those of the cities, were revised to reflect the public's continuing desire to plan for growth while protecting the environment. The preservation of open space for recreational purposes was a politically popular issue throughout California in the 1960s. From a 1964 bond act, Yolo County received $300,000 to begin development of its

parks, and two years later the county created a Parks and Recreation Department.

Education was another problem the county faced in the postwar era, when a greater number of students were being educated in outdated, inadequate school buildings. With more families settling in towns, the old one-room schools in the country were becoming obsolete. Unifying the county's schools was a lengthy process, involving the heart-rending process of closing schools and relocating children, but eventually the 31 school districts were reorganized into seven.

The Yolo County Committee on School District Organization took its first serious look at junior college education in the county in 1961. Washington, Davis, and Clarksburg students were included in 1964 in the Los Rios Community College district; Esparto joined Yuba in 1974; Woodland joined Yuba in 1975; and Winters joined Solano in 1974. A Woodland Center of Yuba Community College was built in Woodland in 1976, and

The evening amateur softball game is an American tradition that involves the whole family and considerable civic pride. Here Yolo County Sheriff Forrest Monroe throws out the first ball to start the game at Katy's Place in Capay in 1948. Courtesy, James Monroe, Jr.

extension classes offered by the other community college districts were held in classrooms in existing schools.

Yolo County became the home of a unique educational institution in 1971. On November 3, 1970, 60 Native Americans, who had just occupied Alcatraz Island as a gesture of protest, laid claim to a former U.S. Army Strategic Communication Command facility west of Davis. There they planned to found an institution of higher learning devoted to Mexican-American and American Indian studies. After several months of negotiations, the 640-acre facility was deeded on May 19, 1971, to Deganawidah-Quetzalcoatl University, funded by a $200,000 grant from the federal Office of Economic Opportunity. After several years the Mexican-Americans left, and D-QU, as it is known, developed into the only two-year, accredited postsecondary institution operated solely by and for Native Americans on the West Coast. In 1981 there were 128 students enrolled.

The UC Davis campus, meanwhile, expanded rapidly after World War II. By 1986 it had increased to 3,554 acres.

A major impetus to the campus' growth was the establishment of a four-year degree curriculum and the change of the Farm School Course to a two-year non-degree curriculum. The impact of this change was recalled by Director Walter L. Howard in 1933:

The establishment of lower division instruction in 1922 and the bringing in of a great number of additional instructors, practically doubling the staff, brought about a feeling of institutional pride . . . But the real spiritual life of the institution . . . came with the adoption of the campus building plan . . . , the first concrete evidence we had that the President and the Regents intended to let the institution pursue a normal development.

With the adoption of this first building plan in 1926, the Davis campus became known as the Northern Branch of the College of Agriculture. The administrative headquarters remained in Berkeley until 1952 when Davis

acquired its own chancellor and College of Agriculture.

With increased enrollment after the war, a new campus building program was started and boundaries of the campus were pushed westward. A School of Veterinary Medicine opened in 1948, and a College of Letters and Sciences in 1951. The number of women enrolled at Davis increased significantly when the College of Letters and Sciences was added.

In 1950 the enrollment at Davis was 1,638. A campus general plan prepared in 1954 was designed to accommodate 5,000 students, but after the Regents declared Davis a General Campus of the University of California in 1959, the plan was revised in 1963 for an enrollment of 18,000. Graduate and professional schools of engineering, law, medicine, and administration were added to the cur-

riculum in the 1960s.

Davis' enrollment reached 19,835 in 1987. Growth in enrollment has necessitated construction of housing, teaching, research, administrative, cultural, and recreational facilities. As the UC Davis campus grew, so did the city of Davis. Davis' population, 3,554 in 1950, had grown to 36,640 by 1980.

Davis citizens had long been interested in city planning. The city's first general plan, prepared by Charles H. Cheney and adopted in 1927, concentrated public buildings around a city park at Fifth and B streets. Soon after, Davis Community Church, St. James Catholic Church, a high school (where city government offices were moved in 1981), and Central Park were built around the proposed civic center. Davis City Hall was built in the downtown area in 1938.

The first large-scale housing projects began in 1950 east of the railroad tracks, and the first apartment complex was built in 1951 at Fourth and B streets. By 1961 the city limits had been extended to the north, west, and east.

During the 1960s, 65 subdivisions were built. Between 1952 and 1966 six new elementary schools, two junior high schools, and one senior high school were built. By 1968 the

Left: The developing UC Davis campus (foreground) and its relationship to the city of Davis, with its leap-frogging subdivisions on agricultural land that was annexed in the 1960s, is clearly visible in this 1971 aerial view (looking east toward Sacramento). Old railroad tracks, a new freeway (I-80), and native oak trees in the University Arboretum along Old Putah Creek demonstrate the changes of time. In the distance, farmers are burning grain stubble, preparing for another crop. Courtesy, News Service Office, UC Davis

Below, left: Yolo County, and particularly Davis, values physical fitness. The Ironman Triathlon competition in Hawaii, which involves a 140.6-mile swim-bike-run course, is one of the most challenging of all events for modern athletes. Dave Scott, a Davis athlete, won his fifth world championship Ironman Triathlon in October 1986 in eight hours, 28 minutes, and 37 seconds. Courtesy, Daily Democrat

DAVIS · 1868 · CENTENNIAL YEAR

Davis, the acknowledged bicycle capital of the western world, selected this design by Jane Garritson and Jeanette Copley as its centennial emblem which has since become a local trademark. The City of Davis and the UC Davis campus, with a combined population of 45,000 in 1987, annually registers nearly 30,000 bicycles, and authorities cooperate to provide interlinking bikepaths and develop innovative parking facilities that have become a model for the nation. Courtesy, Davis Area Chamber of Commerce

population was 20,100 and the city covered an area of five square miles, some still in agricultural production.

Despite the city's rapid growth, major traffic congestion has been alleviated by buses and bicycles. Unitrans, the locally owned bus system, was initiated in 1968 when the Associated Students of UCD purchased two red double-decked London buses to transport students who lived off-campus. By 1987 Unitrans, cosponsored by the city and the student association, operated a fleet of 21 buses driven by trained students.

Davis' innovative bikeways—28 miles of separate bike lanes on city streets and 16 miles of bicycle paths—were developed in the late 1960s. In 1967 Davis became the first city in the nation to construct a bikeway on its thoroughfares.

Not only has Davis been called a "City of Bicycles," it has also gained a reputation as a "Solar City." An Energy Conservation Building Ordinance, adopted in 1975, required north-south orientation of all new construction and encouraged the use of solar heating devices. Solar panels began to appear

on the south-facing slopes of many older buildings as well.

As the city and the university continued to grow rapidly, a new general plan was adopted in 1973 that strove to limit and control the city's future growth. In 1987 the city's population was 41,320, and Davis citizens, faced with strong new pressures to grow, were again revising the general plan.

Like Davis, Woodland also began to change after World War II. During the war, Woodland was a quiet, prosperous town of about 6,637 people. When the war ended, the city applied for federal funds to build 250 houses for returning veterans. In April 1947 the city passed a $400,000 bond issue for an expanded city hall and jail, larger fire station, expanded water system, expanded sewer system, and a community swimming pool. Woodland continued to grow during the 1950s. In 1958 the city adopted a master plan which zoned areas for residential and commercial development around town and for industrial development on the northeast edge of town.

During the 1960s new industries were encouraged, including Mobil Chemical and several manufacturers of mobile homes. These newcomers joined the agriculture-related businesses that had traditionally been the basis of the town's economy.

By 1970 Woodland's population had more than doubled since 1950, to 20,677. During the next decade more city services were developed, the city's master plan was revised, more schools were built, new parks were developed, city hall was remodeled, large shopping centers sprang up, and the northeast industrial area expanded.

In 1980 the town's population had grown to 30,500. The land within the city limits had tripled since 1950, to 6.69 square miles. There were 12 elementary schools, two junior high schools, one high school, three private schools, and one community college campus.

In 1983 the elegant county courthouse, which had graced Courthouse Square since 1917, had a new neighbor on Second Street, the Erwin E. Meier County Administration

Building. In 1986, when the County Fair Mall opened on the south edge of town, downtown businesspeople redoubled their efforts to maintain Main Street as the commercial center of town.

In the 1950s many of Woodland's old homes and businesses were torn down in the name of "progress." By the 1970s there was a renewed interest in preserving and renovating some of the city's graceful nineteenth-century homes and downtown commercial buildings. The Yolo County Historical Society purchased the 1896 Woodland Opera House in 1971. Made a State Historic Park in 1980, the building was restored for use as a theater and museum.

East Yolo—the unincorporated communities of Broderick, Bryte, and West Sacramento—was the fastest-growing area in Yolo County immediately after World War II. In 1940, 5,185 people inhabited the 23 square miles that lay between the Sacramento Weir on the north and Shangri-la Slough on the south. By 1950 the population doubled to 11,225; by 1960 it doubled again, to 25,032. By 1980 the population had dropped to 24,720.

New residents flocked into the area for a number of reasons. After the war, military personnel, commercial and industrial developers, and state employees and their families—all looking for inexpensive, available land for housing and development—found what they were looking for across the Sacramento River from the state capital.

Another reason for East Yolo's rapid growth was the development of the Sacramento-Yolo Port in West Sacramento. After many studies and many set-backs, Congress approved federal participation in a Deep Water Channel Project for the area in 1946. Construction of the port involved a 42.8-mile ship channel, 30 feet deep, from Suisun Bay to West Sacramento; a 60-acre deep-water harbor and turning basin at Lake Washington; port facilities for handling bulk, quasi-bulk and general cargo; and a barge canal between the harbor and the Sacramento River. The project, begun in 1949, was completed in 1963. Construction cost taxpayers approximately $55 million. Port fa-

Huge cranes and belts are used to load bulk cargo into freighters at the Sacramento-Yolo Port. Although the port is 79 nautical miles from the Pacific Ocean, it can accommodate ocean-going ships, thanks to the construction of a 30-foot-deep ship channel and basin large enough for large ships to turn around in. The port opened on July 29, 1963. Courtesy, The News-Ledger

cilities were expanded in the 1960s and 1970s, and a large industrial district was developed next to the port. By 1980 it was estimated that the port and adjacent industrial park had generated 7,200 new jobs and $135 million for the local economy. In 1986 Congress approved deepening the ship channel to 35 feet.

In 1959, while the port was under construction, the county prepared a master plan for the area's development. (East Yolo did not have a city government to manage its explosive growth. The County of Yolo and a large number of special districts provided the services required by this urbanized area.) Churches, stores, banks, shopping centers, and post offices were built as the population grew. Between 1949 and 1962 nine new elementary schools were built, as were East Yolo's first two high schools.

The four water companies that provided water to the area were merged into one in the 1960s, and sold to Citizens Utility Company of Connecticut in 1968. In 1976 the Community Services District was formed to consolidate the three local sanitary districts and to construct and maintain local public parks and recreational facilities. The district was also charged with taking over the water company, something it finally achieved in 1983 after lengthy litigation.

Home rule for East Yolo had been debated since the 1860s. The rapid growth of the postwar period, and increasing frustration with the level of services provided by the county and by special districts, gave the issue of incorporation more compelling importance after the 1960s. Even so, local voters rejected incorporation in 1968 and 1972. Then on June 3, 1986, incorporation was approved and the new city was given the name West Sacramento.

As the cities of Yolo County grew, so did its road system. Once wartime gas rationing was ended and new automobiles were available to buy and drive, millions of Californians took to the highways. Yolo County began to upgrade its county roads and bridges, and over the years the state improved its six highways in the county—Highways 16,

84, 128, 113, 99W, and 45.

Construction on sections of America's interstate, limited access freeways through Yolo County began in 1940. That year the section of US 40 that passed through Davis and the university was replaced by a four-lane divided freeway south of the city. Planned construction in 1950 of a new link of US 40 in West Sacramento caused an outpouring of protest by local residents and businesses. The four-lane, divided highway was completed in 1954. (Local businesspeople immediately formed the Yolo County Hotel-Motel Association "to promote and encourage the waning business of East Yolo" caused by the rerouted traffic.)

Two years later these sections of US 40 were designated part of Interstate 80, the major east-west transcontinental freeway. To carry I-80 over the Sacramento River, the Pioneer Bridge was opened in 1966. The Yolo Causeway was replaced by a double bridge in 1963 and widened in 1984. When a bypass freeway was constructed around the city of Sacramento to connect with I-80 in West Sacramento, the Bryte Bend Bridge was built over the Sacramento River in 1971.

In the 1960s the first north-south interstate freeway in the western part of the county became I-505. The new four-lane divided freeway bypassed Dunnigan, Zamora, Madison, and Winters entirely, and created an ugly gash in the gentle terrain of Fairview, Hungry Hollow, and the Dunnigan Hills.

The second north-south freeway, I-5, cut the town of Zamora in two. Zamora had been impacted by transportation elements before. Its original name, Black's, had been changed by a railway official when the town's founder, James Black, died in 1906. The town was renamed "Zamora," after a town in western Spain.

Zamora's most important building—the Odd Fellows Hall—was relocated in 1949 when Highway 99W was improved. And in 1969, Zamora's commercial district was completely eliminated when the new I-5 freeway was built through the middle of town. A new town hall, Odd Fellows Hall and post office, and a firehouse were built soon afterwards, but all that remained of old Zamora were a Bemmerly warehouse and St. Agnes Catholic Church on the east, and the Zamora school and six residences west of the new freeway.

The new I-5 passed to the west of Yolo, across the northeastern corner of Woodland, and then east toward Sacramento County. A new freeway bridge was built over the Sacramento River at Elkhorn, which opened in 1969. The Elkhorn Bridge replaced the Elkhorn Ferry, Yolo's last ferry across the Sacramento River. The bridge's name was changed to Vietnam Veterans Bridge in 1986.

* * *

Since its earliest days, Yolo County has been a land of changing patterns. The most basic and important patterns are those made by agriculture. There are also the patterns made by the transportation routes, while cities, towns, and communities have left their imprints too.

When Yolo County was established in 1850, there were about 1,000 people living on its approximately 1,000 square miles. In 1980

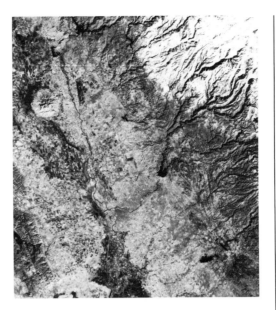

the county had 113,374 people, most of them living in urban areas. The larger cities —Davis, Woodland, and West Sacramento —have grown rapidly, as has the University of California at Davis. The city of Winters remains a small town and some of the isolated rural areas, like Hungry Hollow and Oat Valley, have changed little since the nineteenth century. But there are indications of great changes ahead, and new patterns will surely be carved on the land.

Left: A view of Yolo County from outer space, taken in 1973, presents a unique perspective of its place in the Sacramento Valley and of the designs of natural and man-made waterways. Distinctive features are the craggy Sutter Buttes (upper left); Lake Berryessa and Suisun Bay (lower left); the meandering Sacramento River, lineal deep-water ship channel, and leveed Colusa and Yolo drainage basins (center); and Folsom Lake on the American River (center right). Courtesy, News Service Office, UC Davis

Below, left: This 1985 map illustrates Yolo County's irregular shape, the imprint of roads and freeways, and the location of towns and cities. Compared to the first county map of 1871, the changes are numerous, but the first recorded design on the land, William Gordon's Rancho Quesesosi of 1842 (shown as a rectangle on Cache Creek), is still clearly visible at the county's center point. Courtesy, Yolo County Community Development Agency

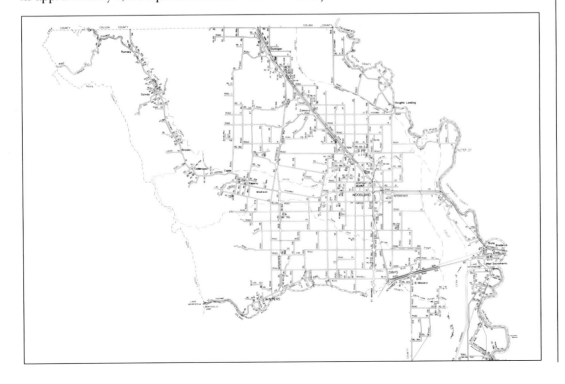

A field of wheat, pictured against rolling hills and outlined by native oak trees in the western Yolo County vicinity of Madison and Esparto, gives a sense of the beauty and fertility of the land which has bound man to the soil for countless generations. Courtesy, Harvey Himelfarb

8

PARTNERS IN PROGRESS

From the businesses, the agricultural life, the institutions, and the people of Yolo County, a pervading theme emerges, develops, and keeps recurring: family.

Many diverse ethnic groups have made their lives from this fertile land at various times in the area's history. Many of their descendants remain today to carry on traditions and enhance the community. Yolo County has many two- and three-generation businesses that keep the old feelings of family alive. Even if young people decide to sample lifestyles elsewhere, a surprising number of them come back to stay. Proud of the contributions of their forebears, sons and daughters commonly give community service through the same organizations with which their fathers and mothers were affiliated.

One can visit an automobile dealer, rice mill, bank, real estate company, hardware business, the local newspaper, or a medical practice and often learn that the owner or manager is carrying on a business or profession started by parents, or perhaps even grandparents. Old-timers may drop in to reminisce, and everyone is on a first-name basis. People dress informally and don't stand on ceremony.

Business owners and managers arriving from somewhere else are likely to get as involved in the county's history as if they'd grown up here.

Even when a company or institution isn't owned or operated by a family, businesses come to seem like families more often than not. Hospital personnel enjoy working together and they treat their patients in the old-fashioned way—like friends. Many employees have been with their companies for 30 or 40 years. If there's illness in an employee's family the boss knows about it, and helps if he can.

Big-city anonymity has no place in Yolo County. Bank tellers take pains to remember people's names. People walk down the street and speak to one another, whether or not they've met, and go out of their way to help others. People care.

Around the University of California at Davis are the families of scholars from all over the world. Strangers in a strange land, they soon learn they're not alone, as caring citizens help them learn English and give assistance in many other ways. In return the visitors share their culture and tradition with Yoloans.

Agriculture is, of course, the lifeblood of Yolo County, and no one, no matter what his occupation, can ever take the California bounty for granted. It has been the foundation for a great university and for a way of life.

The county's peaceful farmlands, with their rolling hills and miles of flat land stretching off toward the mountains or the Sacramento River Delta, can offer renewal after the most stressful day. On summer nights the bright stars shine a welcome from as far as the eye can see.

Volunteers guard the county's traditions and history through a number of historical preservation groups. Other volunteers serve the disadvantaged, the emotionally disturbed, the terminally ill, or the physically handicapped. Still others promote quality education and the arts. Businesses large and small contribute many thousands of dollars each year to community causes.

The organizations whose histories are related on the following pages have chosen to support this important literary and civic project. These businesses, institutions of learning, services, and associations that comprise the community of business, along with the local citizens, have made Yolo County an excellent place to live and work.

YOLO COUNTY HISTORICAL SOCIETY

The Yolo County Historical Society, first founded in 1948, has its own history, that of working to save important historic buildings for public use, then often turning them over to a government body better able to restore and maintain them.

The first building preserved by the society, the old Springlake School-house, purchased in 1950 and moved to the Yolo County Fairgrounds by the County Fair Board, is still maintained by the society as a small museum, featuring exhibits of old photographs and other artifacts each year during fair time.

In 1971 the society purchased the

RIGHT: The Springlake Schoolhouse was purchased for $350 by the Yolo County Historical Society in 1950, and has served ever since as a small museum during the Yolo County Fair.

BELOW: The Yolo County Historical Society spearheaded a fund drive in 1973 that led to the purchase of the old Gibson Mansion, and its restoration to serve as the Yolo County Museum.

The Woodland Opera House, once the scene of gala performances, stood empty and neglected for almost 60 years until it was rescued by the Yolo County Historical Society.

sturdy but neglected Woodland Opera House, vacant since 1913, for $12,000. Community fund drives were organized, local legislators gave vital support, and, with one million dollars from state appropriations, $400,000 from the National Preservation Act, and $70,000 from the City of Woodland, restoration became possible.

In 1979 the property became the Woodland Opera House Historic Park. The state supervises restoration but delegates operation to the City of Woodland, administered by a local board of trustees. The building has been expanded and significantly restored, but much needed work

remains to be done.

In 1965 the Yolo County Historical Society saw the old Gibson Mansion as a possible permanent museum, and by 1968 started a museum fund. Five years later the society led an effort to persuade the board of supervisors to allocate $20,000 in Revenue Sharing Funds, and in 1974 the supervisors named an advisory committee.

The Gibson Mansion was purchased for $19,000 in 1975, and the Yolo County Museum Association was

formed that same year to promote development and raise supporting funds. A separate nine-member board operates the museum for the county. Society volunteers donate the proceeds from a dessert booth at the museum's annual May Festival.

To inform residents of the county's colorful past and promote the preservation of important landmarks, the society sponsors monthly programs about the area's history and publishes booklets on historical subjects. The authors of *Land of Changing Patterns* are preparing a series of minihistories of specific county areas to be published by the society, which also is sponsoring a series of plates featuring historic buildings.

When the first historical society was organized in 1948 by W.G. Bernhardt, 13 charter members paid dues of one dollar. By 1950 there were more than 80 members; they raised $350 in a community drive to purchase the Springlake Schoolhouse.

Then the society was disbanded until 1963, when it was reorganized by Vivian Douglas, county librarian, and the Reverend E.E. Zimmerman of Winters. This time 256 charter members paid dues of $2.50, and the society kept going. Today there are more than 300 members. The first officers were Mrs. J. Dudley Stephens, Esparto, president, and Zimmerman, Joann Larkey, Stuart B. Waite, and Dick Blanchard.

In 1986 the Yolo County Historical Society contributed to the restoration of Capay Cemetery near Esparto, and Mary's Chapel and Cemetery in Yolo. The society's response to the vandalism of these landmarks was typical of a group of citizens who are working to preserve history, rather than to destroy it.

YOLO COUNTY SUPERINTENDENT OF SCHOOLS

Many of the schools' names came from nature, such as Willow Spring, Apricot, Cottonwood, Pleasant Prairie, Buckeye, Clover, Cache Creek, Pine Grove, and Riverbank. Other names had themes like Excelsior, Liberty, and Enterprise, while still others honored places, presidents, and prominent people.

In 1855, when the office of Yolo County Superintendent of Schools was established, the county was dotted with school districts, many containing a single one-room school-

The Rhoda Maxwell Primary School (1915-1967) in Woodland, located on the original site of the Walnut Street School (1887-1912), housed the Woodland School District offices from 1967 to 1978, and since then has held the offices of the Yolo County Superintendent of Schools.

The Greengate Center for Exceptional Children, providing day classes for children with severe mental, physical, or learning handicaps, is just one of several special educational services offered by the county superintendent's office.

house. Today there are five unified school districts, and while each could be thought of as independent, behind them all is the office of the county superintendent.

Countywide supervision of schools dates from May 3, 1852, when "an act to establish a system of common schools" was mandated by state legislation, creating the public schools of Yolo County and defining the duties of the county superintendent.

Until 1855 the supervision of schools was an extra duty of the county assessor; then S.N. Mering became the first actual Yolo County Superintendent of Schools. He was to personally visit each school each year, generally supervise all schools, and give "such aid and counsel as may be important to the prosperity of the schools." He also was to see that examination of teachers was "sufficiently rigid and thorough," and was to disperse school funds among the districts "in proportion to the number of white children residing therein."

In 1885 the 49 school districts had 69 teachers. Capay Valley's Canon School, still standing, operated for 100 years, until 1962. However, consolidations continued until today there are five districts: Davis, Esparto, Washington, Winters, and Woodland.

As the intermediate educational unit between the State Department of Education and the districts, the superintendent's office keeps districts informed on legislation, arranges staff and faculty workshops, helps with legal services, processes teacher credentials, supervises school district elections, and arbitrates in unresolved disputes with districts, among other duties.

Local districts handle such services as health screening programs and learning disability instruction,

with the help of county schools, but the county schools provide transportation and offer several day classes for children with severe mental, physical, or learning handicaps.

General education programs offer vocational, career, and job placement services to high school students; classes at the county juvenile hall; individualized academic and counseling programs for minors with adjustment problems; and academic instruction, counseling, childbirth preparation, and basic parenting skills to pregnant teenagers and young mothers.

Current superintendent John Graf states that the "overall mission of the Yolo County Office of Education is to provide and promote, in cooperation with school districts, educational programs and services to students in Yolo County that are of high quality and cost effective, and to function as an intermediate unit for the State Department of Education."

As a Yolo County native, Graf feels related to those long-ago parents in remote areas, who worked together to provide schools and teachers for their children.

W.J. BLEVINS MEDICAL GROUP, INC.

The W.J. Blevins Medical Group, Inc., has its roots in the practice of Dr. William J. Blevins, Sr., who with other early physicians established the first real hospital in Yolo County and set the standard for future quality medical care. Eventually he formed his own medical group and was joined in 1937 by his son, Dr. W.J. Blevins, Jr., who retired in 1977 and lives in Woodland.

After graduating in 1898 from Barnes Medical College in Missouri, the senior Blevins had come home to Mendocino County to treat his first patient—for impetigo. He set up his first local practice in Madison and practiced briefly in Winters. Then he bought out a practice in Blacks (now Zamora), paying $84 for the retiring doctor's horse and buggy with medical equipment thrown in.

In 1900 Blevins established a Woodland office above the old Leithold's Drug Store, worked at the County Hospital (more like a poorhouse), and became county health

The Blevinses, senior and junior, practiced medicine in the Porter Building on Woodland's Main Street for more than 40 years before moving the practice to its present location. The Porter Building is on the National Register of Historic Places.

officer. The latter job included examinations of schoolchildren; but one parent wrote him that spiders in the school outhouses were a greater menace than any germs he might find.

In his private practice, he delivered babies in homes—a doctor might have to stay all day and night for a $20 fee. Blevins charged $1.50 for an office visit and $2.50 for a regular house call.

The doctor told colleagues at a 1949 meeting that for house calls in summer, the roads were fair; in winter they were "terrible," and he'd need a team instead of one horse. Once he took the electric train on a call; when trying to flag down the train for the return trip, his lantern signal was missed in the heavy fog and he walked the trestle on his way home. Flooding caused many calls to be made by boat. Finally Blevins and other doctors built a small rural telephone system to better communicate with their patients.

Later his association with doctors C.H. Fairchild, F.R. Fairchild, and H.D. Lawhead would become the basis for the current Woodland Clinic Medical Group, which built a hospital/clinic and encouraged the community's involvement in fund raising for a nonprofit community hospital.

After serving in the Army during World War I, Blevins and Dr. Fred Fairchild returned to the group practice, but in 1932, when effects of the Depression threatened to close

their Woodland Clinic Hospital, Dr. Blevins opened his own offices in the Porter Building, moving in 1974 to Three Court Street. The senior Dr. Blevins died in 1953. Other notable physicians no longer in the practice are John O'Hara, Roy A. Neumann, and Richard P. Armstrong.

The W.J. Blevins Medical Group consists today of Dr. James T. Barrett and Dr. Kenneth W. Patric, Jr., with Dr. Charles Derby as associate. All are residency trained and board certified in family practice.

Many staff members perform important and stabilizing roles under the direction of office manager Yvonne Hannon. Two of them, Diane Hawke and John Russell, have served 27 years, and Dedi Zane has served 14 years.

The full-service family practice remains committed to both the personal caring of the "old-time family doctor" and the scientific expertise of the present.

Dr. William J. Blevins, Sr., started practicing medicine in Yolo County in 1898, and participated in the evolution over some 50 years from horse-and-buggy medicine to sophisticated clinic and hospital care.

Dr. William J. Blevins, Jr., now retired and living in Woodland, joined his father in the W.J. Blevins Medical Group in 1937 and cared for its patients for 40 years, continuing the tradition of personal and caring family practice.

DAVIS LUMBER & HARDWARE COMPANY

Davis Lumber & Hardware Company is the oldest Davis business still in existence. As its sole owners since 1962, the Anderson family has turned a small lumber and hardware company into a large multidepartment store, selling everything from bolts to boards to boutique items.

John B. Anderson and his younger brother, Andrew Gordon ("Gordon" or "A.G."), came to Davis about 1900, and each went into business. Gordon Anderson became a partner in a haberdashery and general mercantile business on G Street. "J.B." was the first mayor of Davis, and later, in the 1920s and 1930s, Gordon was mayor for 13 years.

In 1909 Essie Powers arrived in town to work at University Farm and later at the Davis Lumber Company. She and Gordon married, and their son, Donald George Anderson, was

In 1914 Gordon Anderson (behind the counter) and his wife, Essie, purchased a hardware store on G Street, across from where the Davis Lumber & Hardware Company is now. The store carried everything from garden hoses to Cannon Ball wagons.

born in 1917. In 1914 the Andersons had bought a hardware store on G Street, renaming it A.G. Anderson Hardware.

On June 22, 1962, Donald, Dora, and Essie Anderson purchased the Davis Lumber Company from the

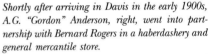

Shortly after arriving in Davis in the early 1900s, A.G. "Gordon" Anderson, right, went into partnership with Bernard Rogers in a haberdashery and general mercantile store.

Robie family, operating it together until Essie died at age 94, on November 14, 1978, having worked up until a few days before her death. Don and Dora Anderson then operated the store until Don's death on June 7, 1986. They'd been joined by daughters Jennifer Anderson in 1982 and Mary Jo Hoes in 1983.

The store now has, in addition to lumber, paint, and hardware sections, a garden shop, nursery, pet and feed sections, art supplies, landscaping materials, rental equipment, and an expanded housewares section.

Mary Jo Hoes and Jennifer Anderson, who co-manage the store, added a small museum to display things like old cash registers and nail barrels, there when their father and their grandfather were first in business. Says Hoes, "We keep finding things in the back room."

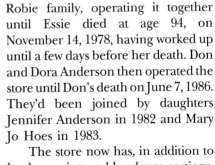

WOODLAND CLINIC MEDICAL GROUP

At the turn of the century many physicians served a small Yolo County population; but it was difficult for doctors to reach their patients, most of whom lived widely scattered over miles of farm and ranch land.

Thanks to the vision of a few medical and nursing pioneers, the creation of the Woodland Clinic, and a series of hospital buildings leading to today's still-growing Woodland Memorial Hospital, made the delivery of adequate, quality medical care a primary community concern.

As in many rural communities, physicians had traveled by horse and buggy, often over flooded roads, to treat the sick in their homes, deliver babies in bedrooms, and frequently perform surgery under adverse conditions. In those days there were outbreaks of typhoid, diphtheria, or malaria.

If an operation could be planned in advance, a nurse might move into the home a couple of days ahead and prepare for surgery, usually on the kitchen table in a well-lighted room, doing her best to make the area aseptic.

Then, in 1907, the Woodland Sanitarium, immediate predecessor of the Woodland Clinic Hospital and Medical Group, was opened by registered nurse Kathleen McConnell. With her two sisters, also nurses, she rented a two-story home at 110 College Street and converted it to a facility with nine beds and a surgery unit that was immediately welcomed by physicians. In 1909, when more beds were needed, a small adjacent cottage on the corner of College and Clover

streets was rented. From this small seed the Woodland Clinic Medical Group grew.

In 1911 four Woodland physicians, Dr. Fred Fairchild, his brother Dr. Chester Fairchild, Dr. Hiram Lawhead, and Dr. William Blevins, Sr., merged their practices and became the founding fathers of the medical facilities to come when they bought the sanitarium and also a small lot on the corner of Third and Cross streets, planned as the site of a new general hospital. Following World War I, in April 1920, two more parcels immediately north of the hospital site were purchased, and construction began.

With the new building under way the founders started actively organizing a clinic group of physicians, and this group eventually resulted in Woodland Clinic, Inc. By 1925 it was obvious that more hospital facilities were needed, and a three-story wing on Cross Street was completed in 1928.

Many changes were occurring in medicine during those early years, and the Woodland Clinic became well known in Northern California for the quality of its combined practice, attracting other physicians until it was one of the largest physician groups in California.

The founders of the Woodland Clinic Medical Group were Dr. Fred Fairchild (above left), Dr. Chester Fairchild (left), Dr. Hiram Lawhead (above), and Dr. William Blevins (right).

Woodland Clinic and Hospital on Third Street as it looked in 1928.

During the 1930s the name of the Woodland Sanitarium was changed to the Woodland Clinic Hospital. The hospital was almost lost to the community during the Depression, when the Yolo County Savings Bank foreclosed over an indebtedness of $135,000. The hospital didn't lack patients—the patients just couldn't pay. But the bank had serious problems running the hospital and finally decided to return it to the management of the medical group. Businessmen in the community helped the group liquidate the clinic's debts by 1936.

The next significant expansion of the hospital was made in 1958, when a new surgical and maternity wing replaced the older units, which then became clinic physicians' offices.

Dr. Fred Fairchild believed the art of medicine must be a collaboration between the medical community and the general community; he understood that to function successfully a medical group of diverse specialties must prioritize group interests over personal interest. Clinic doctors bore their fair shares of the emergency loads and calls to outlying areas, regardless of their specialties. New physicians had to demonstrate the ability to work in harmony with their

buildings surrounding a large and pleasant courtyard at 1207 Fairchild Court, next to Woodland Memorial Hospital. The clinic also has satellite offices in Davis and Sacramento.

More than 70 physicians in some 30 specialty departments own and operate the clinic, providing health care at the forefront of medical technology, with many advances such as cardiac catheterization and laser

The Woodland Clinic today.

colleagues, and this is still true today.

Fairchild believed these attributes, offered collectively, made it possible to effectively serve the community. In turn, the community responded with an outpouring of support when clinic physicians and community leaders moved toward changing the status of the Woodland Clinic Hospital to the nonprofit Woodland Memorial Hospital. The facility was, in effect, being given to the community by Woodland Clinic doctors.

As this changeover occurred in 1960, a community fund-raising effort was launched to build a large, modern facility at Gibson Road and Cottonwood Street. (The history of the present Woodland Memorial Hospital follows this story.)

The Woodland Clinic Medical Group pays tribute to its longtime business manager, Dan Kelley, for his leadership in developing the clinic and its present complex of

surgery. All departments provide 24-hour on-call care. And as in the early days, patients come to the clinic not only from the local area, but from all over the West.

The Women's Care Center, opened in March 1986, offers prenatal care, infertility and premenstrual syndrome counseling, osteoporosis screening, and screening for breast cancer, as well as a library and educational video material.

The separate, nonprofit Woodland Clinic Research and Education Foundation seeks to advance the science of medicine and improve patient and physician education.

In January 1987 a historical plaque was presented to the Woodland Clinic by the Woodland Memorial Hospital Board of Directors, honoring the clinic's 75 years of service to the widespread community.

WOODLAND MEMORIAL HOSPITAL

The history of the modern and progressive Woodland Memorial Hospital in Woodland is intertwined with that of the old—and still active—Woodland Clinic; its forerunner, the Woodland Sanitarium; and the Woodland Clinic Hospital and Medical Group. The current hospital evolved from some 75 years of dedicated medical practice always motivated by the desire to serve the

Nurses relax on the porch of the Woodland Sanitarium, established in 1907 by registered nurse Kathleen McConnell as a facility for surgery and patient care. Before that doctors usually performed surgery on kitchen tables in patients' homes.

community. With this legacy Woodland Memorial continues the tradition with state-of-the-art inpatient, outpatient, and educational services to a growing community.

(A history of the Woodland Clinic's role in establishing the quality medical care and facilities that led to Woodland Memorial Hospital is given on the two preceding pages.)

It was a happy day for the community when ground was broken for the present Woodland Memorial Hospital in the early 1960s. In the foreground (from left) are Edna Grimsrud, registered nurse; Kenneth Lowe, hospital board member; Virginia Kelley, auxiliary president; and Dr. O.C. Railsback, hospital board member.

In 1959 Woodland Clinic Hospital physicians decided the community would be better served by a not-for-profit hospital. After a year of meetings in which the corporation, medical staff, and organization of the hospital were planned, the Woodland Clinic Memorial Hospital received nonprofit hospital status on September 1, 1960. At that point the clinic doctors, in effect, donated all the assets of the hospital they had owned to the community. The name "Memorial" was intended to memorialize area residents, and soon the word "Clinic" was dropped because clinic doctors no longer owned the hospital.

Woodland Clinic physicians continued their professional affiliation with the hospital, and at the same time other physicians from throughout the larger community joined the staff of Woodland Memorial Hospital.

In 1960 five laymen and four physicians became the first directors of the new corporation; they were Neal Chalmers, Phil Collins, Kenneth Lowe, Sid Epperson, James Wilson, Dr. Robert Burns, Dr. Woodring

The modern, not-for-profit Woodland Memorial Hospital, completed in 1967 with a major addition in 1980, is the result of a longtime communitywide commitment to quality medical care in the Woodland area.

Pearson, Dr. O.C. Railsback, and Dr. Richard Cundiff.

The following year the Woodland Memorial Hospital Auxiliary was formed. Its first president was Martha Sans, assisted by officers Jean Fiddyment, Anne Barron, Donna Scarlett, Christine Berettoni, and Etta Van Zee; and active members Bessie Adams and Phyllis Stoeven. The auxiliary continues today, operating the hospital's gift shop, sponsoring fund-raising events, and providing volunteer services that offer extra amenities to patients.

Almost immediately after organizing, the corporation's board of directors decided to expand the hospital facilities by moving to a new, 20-acre site at the corner of Gibson Road and Cottonwood Street, where a large, modern hospital could be built. Together with the Woodland Clinic, under the leadership of its administrator, Dan Kelley, the directors launched a communitywide fund-raising campaign for the $4-million, 113-bed facility. Clinic doctors led the way with their personal contributions.

The areawide campaign raised one-third of the funds needed, with the remainder coming through a federal Hill-Burton Grant and from borrowing through bonds. The facility was completed in April 1967.

The Woodland Clinic Medical Group, which by now had 55 physicians, relocated adjacent to the hospital, creating a sophisticated and comprehensive health care complex that also included dental offices.

The combination of major gifts and grass-roots giving began a tradition of support from the broader community—including towns some distance away. Soon this support was further encouraged by the Woodland Memorial Hospital Foundation, begun in 1967 by the hospital board; Woodland Clinic physicians; Dan Kelley, by now the hospital administrator; and concerned citizens who wanted to assure the continued excellence of health care practiced in Woodland for so many years.

Today, as then, the foundation, one of the earliest hospital foundations to be formed in Northern California and in the United States, is dedicated to improving health care for all people through the support of hospital programs and services. To address the need for more emphasis on outpatient and diagnostic services,

These technicians in the laboratory of the old Woodland Clinic Hospital were dedicated and thorough, but by today's standards their facilities left much to be desired. The photo probably was taken in the early 1930s.

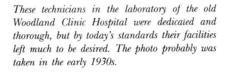

and better emergency facilities, the hospital, in 1976, started building a $2.7-million emergency/outpatient department, also increasing patient beds to 122. Community contributions provided more than one-third of the funding for this expansion, which was completed in 1980.

During the 1980s, as hospitals were experiencing reduced outlays for hospital care from third-party payors and from Medicare fixed payments, significant but costly advances were being made in medical technology. Woodland Memorial Hospital has been meeting the challenge in the mid-1980s by balancing cost efficiency with its traditional quality care that includes a wide range of high-technology, life-saving treatments and services such as laser surgery, a multipurpose cardiac catheterization laboratory, a mobile magnetic resonance imaging unit to produce detailed diagnostic images without radiation, and a mobile lithotripter to noninvasively crush kidney stones.

Adding to existing services, the hospital initiated a specialized physical therapy program for the treatment of arthritis and sports and orthopedic injuries. The outpatient surgery department was further ex-

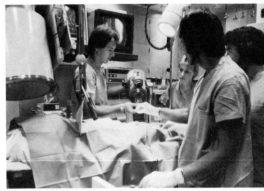

Medical personnel meet the challenge of 1980s technology in the multipurpose cardiac catheterization laboratory, which not only aids in the diagnosis and treatment of cardiac conditions but also enhances sophisticated radiological and urological studies.

panded, and a highly trained Home Health nursing staff extended care to patients in their own homes. The obstetrics department expanded to meet the growing demand for family-style childbirth in homelike delivery rooms. Community health classes were instituted to help people deal with problems related to smoking cessation, stress management, childbirth, and cancer.

As the populations of Yolo and its surrounding counties grow closer together, Woodland Memorial Hospital is becoming part of an expanding Sacramento Valley health network expected to lead to cooperative efforts such as regionalized patient referrals, eldercare programs, and other affiliations to improve specialized services.

The Woodland Clinic Hospital at Third and Cross streets, with its three-story extension, completed in 1928, was used until the current Woodland Memorial Hospital was completed in 1967. The extension is now the Woodland Skilled Nursing Facility.

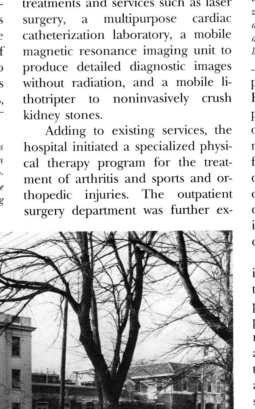

BANK OF WOODLAND

Although one of several banks located on the west side of Woodland, Bank of Woodland is different from all the others. This is because of its emphasis on small to medium-size business banking, says the institution's president and chief executive officer, Roger Kohlmeier. Bank of Woodland also is the only still-existing bank founded and headquartered in Yolo County. Of the approximately 525 shareholders, most are local residents.

Located at 120 West Court Street, the institution opened for business on January 10, 1983, and is operated by 12 local directors: Kohlmeier, Thomas Atkinson II, Robert Buttcane, Scott Carson, Milton Lee, James Ocheltree, and Gary Wirth, all of Woodland; Daniel Dowling, Frederick Sobeck, and board chairman William Streng, all of Davis; Robert Nickum, of Dixon; and Arthur Traugh, of Sacramento.

These business and professional men, all of whom are active in volunteer service to their communities, saw the need for a local bank that would serve small to medium-size businesses, professional people, and farmers. All of the institution's services are oriented toward such clients, rather than consumer oriented in the tradition of most banks. Although Bank of Woodland is a full-service bank, it discourages "walk-in" customers by setting a high minimum-opening balance. The facility's business is not handling auto loans or home improvement loans, says Kohlmeier, although it will provide such services to its regular clients as needed.

"At inception," Kohlmeier adds, "we recognized the need to establish in Yolo County a business-oriented financial institution. And the deposits we take in stay in Yolo County, going

Roger Kohlmeier, president and chief executive officer of Bank of Woodland.

into local businesses and enterprises."

The board of directors also sets aside a substantial percentage of profits for charitable donations in the community.

Kohlmeier believes that a locally based banking institution can be more responsive to credit requests, act more quickly, and be more flexible and less structured in outlook. Often customers do not even have to come in—much business is done through couriers who go to their offices—but when they do visit the bank, they receive special treatment. There are no tellers' windows or lines in the handsomely appointed main room. Rather, business is done at desks with comfortable chairs, and in private offices when necessary.

Exactly one year after Bank of Woodland opened, a branch was established in Davis. Expansion plans for the Woodland office are currently under way, to make more space for the institution's approximately 40 employees, tripled from the original 13 in just four years.

Founding directors of Bank of Woodland celebrate the bank's approval to organize in 1982. Seated (from left) are Roger Kohlmeier, president and chief executive officer; and William Streng, board chairman. Standing (from left) are Thomas Atkinson II, Robert Buttcane, Robert Nickum, Frederick Sobeck, and Gary Wirth. Not shown are Scott Carson, Milton Lee, Elmer McNece, and Arthur Traugh.

Just four years after Bank of Woodland opened at 120 West Court Street, plans for an expansion were under way. Architect Gary Wirth's rendering shows how the building will look after completion.

WEST SACRAMENTO LAND COMPANY

ABOVE: Car 26 arrives at the West Sacramento station opposite new headquarters of the West Sacramento Company at 15th and Jefferson streets. The company built the streetcar line in 1913 to help attract commuters; it was taken over by Sacramento Northern in 1915, operating until 1924.

Helping develop the formerly unincorporated West Sacramento has been West Sacramento Land Company, West Sacramento Company, and finally another West Sacramento Land Company that remains active today.

The original West Sacramento Land Company was organized in 1907 to reclaim East Yolo land from the Sacramento River and develop it. This plan proved too costly; three years later this company dissolved and its assets were transferred to the newly formed West Sacramento Company in exchange for stock in the new firm, then based in the old Kripp family ranch home at what is now the intersection of 15th Street and South River Road.

munity's first part-time postmaster. While managing the West Sacramento Company, Turner formed his own West Sacramento Land Company and started buying parcels from the West Sacramento Company for development of areas such as Westfield Village and Westmore Oaks.

Turner was responsible for the first construction of new single-family homes in the late 1930s on lots of the original development group's subdivision, later adding many more subdivisions.

Turner's business was in the

RIGHT: This 1913 picture shows limousines used by the West Sacramento Company to bring prospective buyers to inspect land, just cleared of its trees and tules.

Arthur F. Turner influenced the opening of a local branch of Anglo California National Bank in 1952. Turner's new offices and the bank shared space in this new building at Merkley Avenue and Jefferson Boulevard.

In 1913 Arthur Franklin Turner, the son of California pioneers, became company bookkeeper. Because family finances were limited, Turner had completed only two years of high school and was helping put a brother through college. After World War I Army service Turner returned to find the company's reclamation efforts more successful. In 1922 he was made general manager, also becoming secretary of Reclamation District 900, established with the help of the firm.

Later he was named the com-

headquarters built in 1913 for the West Sacramento Company, at 15th Street and Jefferson Boulevard. This building served as post office, library, real estate office, polling place, unofficial "city hall," and informal community center. Considered the unofficial mayor, Turner was dubbed "Mister West Sacramento."

Persuading the Anglo California National Bank to open a local branch, Turner initiated a period of expansion in West Sacramento's business district. The bank—later replaced by Wells Fargo Bank—and Turner's new offices shared space in a building he constructed in 1952 at Merkley Avenue and Jefferson Boulevard.

Arthur Turner was a charter

member of several community service organizations and a major contributor to many charities and churches. He also donated considerable land for community needs, the last being for a West Sacramento branch library that bears his name.

Turner died in 1974 at 81 years of age leaving his widow, Edith, sons Howard and John, and daughter Mary Alice Carswell. Both sons are with the firm; Howard became president in 1965. Following his father's lead, he has occupied many of the same community service offices Arthur Turner held. Howard Turner has developed new areas in Southport and several small retail centers. A founding director of the Capitol Bank of Commerce, he served through 1986.

The West Sacramento Land Company is the oldest and largest general brokerage firm in east Yolo. "From the beginning," says Howard Turner, "the firm and its employees have tried to support the community that supports them."

FIRST NORTHERN BANK

Back in 1910 a group of Dixon residents believed they weren't getting the kind of banking services they needed, and decided to do something about it. On January 20 that year 25 people met at the Dixon Alfalfa Land Company.

In the spirit of the independent, do-it-yourself tradition of their farming community, these residents organized a local bank that very day, to be backed with all-local capital and no outside investment or affiliation. Those present elected a board of directors, authorized $100,000 of capital stock, and paid in $60,000 of it. Then they appointed a committee to go to San Francisco for a safe and other necessary supplies.

Twelve days later, on February 1, 1910, Northern Solano Bank was in business in a remodeled former ice cream parlor at approximately 185 North First Street. This humble but forward-looking establishment was the forerunner of the institution now known as First Northern Bank.

New depositors were subtly persuaded with notes in the personal column of the *Dixon Tribune*: ". . . Eighty of your friends have started, why not you?" By March 1910 the bank had 93 accounts with deposits totaling $75,304.55. Two months later there

were 180 depositors and $101,648.84 in accounts.

The first directors were Henry R. Timm, president; Robert E. Lee Stephens, vice-president; H.L. Bissell, secretary/cashier; and J.D. Grady, E.D.N. Lehe, E.R. Watson, W.R. Madden, W.J. Weyand, and J.J. Clark.

By the following year the bank had purchased the "Old Corner" property at North First and B streets. The coveted location was secured by the directors after heated bidding against the Bank of Dixon. A portion of the building was torn down and replaced by a new bank building. The bank's main offices are at the same site today and dominate the block; but back then the bank shared it with a haberdashery, a harness maker, the Wells Fargo Express Company, Pacific Telephone, and a cigar maker.

The following year The First National Bank was established under

Henry R. Timm was the first president of the board of directors when Northern Solano Bank was formed in 1910.

a federal charter, and for the next 43 years it operated under the same roof, and with the same management, as Northern Solano Savings Bank, a state bank. The two banks were consolidated in 1955 as First National Bank of Dixon.

The bank continued to grow and evolve from a small farm bank to a full-service bank addressing the needs of the area's growing population. In 1962, when the bank celebrated its 52nd anniversary, deposits had increased from the original capital stock of $100,000 to $7.7 million. This same year the directors decided to tear down the old bank and construct a new one. In 1970 the bank expanded from its Dixon base by opening its first branch in Winters. The Davis branch followed in 1976, and the West Sacramento branch in 1983, the same year a Real Estate Department was opened in Davis. Vacaville was added to the Solano/Yolo network in 1985.

In 1980 First National Bank of Dixon was converted to a state-chartered institution and became First Northern Bank as it is known today.

Throughout its history First Northern Bank has remained faithful to its roots as a bank formed to address specific personalized needs, and continues to serve such needs for the people of the community.

First Northern Bank's home office as it looks today. The old bank was torn down in the 1960s to make room for this building. John Hamel (right), member of a family with deep roots in both Solano and Yolo counties, is the president, chief executive officer, and a member of the board of directors of First Northern Bank.

WESTERN TITLE INSURANCE COMPANY

In California's early days documents filed on everything from a patent to a property transfer (except for Spanish land grants) were hand-written by an abstractor; these initial records of real property became the beginning documents in a title record chain continuing throughout the life of the properties.

Western Title Insurance Company traces its origin to one C.V. Gillespie, who became, in 1848 during the great influx of gold seekers, a San Francisco notary public and searcher of records.

Two Gillespie clerks, Simpson and Millar, had previously left his employ to form their own company, but later they purchased Gillespie's business. Meanwhile, in 1855 W.H.J. Brooks and one Mr. Saniter opened a title-searching firm in San Francisco; Brooks later became sole owner. In 1863 Brooks became associated with Parker and Rouleau, established in 1862 as Parker, Rouleau and Coombs. Rouleau bought out Brooks in 1868 and ran the business until he died in 1893 and was succeeded by his son, O.A. Rouleau.

The firms of Simpson and Millar and the Rouleau company continued to grow, merging in 1901 to become Rouleau, Simpson & Millar Title Company. Title insurance was not routine then, but as a demand for it arose, Title Insurance and Guaranty Company was formed in 1902 and acquired Rouleau, Simpson & Millar Title Company. O.A. Rouleau became its president.

This successful enterprise faced ruin because of the 1906 San Francisco earthquake and fire, but employees and their wives joined to find a wagon, enter the fire-surrounded business district, and load and push the company records to the yard of

O.A. Rouleau, where the valuable records were buried in a large hole beneath carpets, dirt, and lawn. The Rouleau residence was destroyed; but the buried records remained intact.

Company operations were limited to San Francisco until 1920, when the original Western Title Insurance Company was formed to offer title insurance in the state's rural counties by underwriting agreements with locally owned title abstract firms. As before, the abstractors searched the records, but the accuracy of their work was now backed by the resources of the title insurer.

One such business was Yolo County Title Abstract Co. in Woodland, which had been incorporated in 1895 and consolidated with Woodland Title Company in 1926. Four years later the firm contracted with Title Insurance and Guaranty Company for underwriting, and in 1943 its assets were purchased by Western Title Insurance Company.

In 1951 the latter company was merged into the former under the new name of Western Title Insurance and Guaranty Company; in 1959 the word "Guaranty" was dropped.

After considerable growth in the late 1960s and early 1970s, the firm

The old Foursquare Gospel Church at Second and Court streets in Woodland was taken down in 1956 to make room for the Woodland office of Western Title Insurance Company. Sacramento Northern Railroad trains used to go past the door.

now provides title insurance and escrow services through some 94 offices in 41 counties. Robert H. Morton is corporate chairman and chief executive officer, and John W. Goings is president. Western Title Insurance Company's Woodland and Davis offices are managed by vice-president Charles Kelley.

The Woodland office of Western Title Insurance Company is one of two offices in Yolo County. The Davis office is at 205 E Street.

THE DAVIS ENTERPRISE

A commitment to the local community and to the publishing of local news reflects the belief of the McNaughton family, owners of *The Davis Enterprise*, that community newspapers should truly serve the areas in which they are published. This tradition has been developed through some 70 years and three generations of McNaughtons in

From left are Foy McNaughton, Davis Enterprise publisher and chief executive officer of the three California McNaughton newspapers; Dean McNaughton, chairman of the board of directors of McNaughton Newspapers; and Burt McNaughton, general manager of The Davis Enterprise *and vice-president of McNaughton Newspapers.*

the *Pekin Daily Times* in Illinois, and for the next 60 years McNaughton wrote a daily column for the front page of the paper he edited and published.

He and his wife, "Ceil" (the former Cecille McMillan), raised their five children in Pekin; McNaughton was later to look back on their years together as "60 years of joys!" The family acquired other newspapers along the way, but Pekin was the "home place" for McNaughton, who stayed in the grass roots of the newspaper industry even after being awarded a doctorate from Tri-State College, where he had done his undergraduate work, and a medallion

A commemorative reproduction of the June 3, 1898, edition. The man in the inset photo probably is founder L.A. Eichler.

as an outstanding graduate at his Columbia University 50th class reunion.

When F.F. McNaughton died in 1981 at age 91, three of his children already were involved in newspapering. Son Dean McNaughton had taken over as publisher of the *Pekin Daily Times* in 1952 after his graduation from West Point, and later bought the *Fairfield Daily Republic* in 1960, the *Placerville Mountain Democrat* in 1966, and *The Davis Enterprise* in 1967.

The McNaughtons have owned the *Enterprise* for 20 years, but the newspaper existed long before any

the newspaper business.

The newspaper heritage was established in 1917, when F.F. NcNaughton, who'd been a teacher and high school principal, returned to college at Columbia University for a master's degree in journalism, worked three years on the *New York Tribune*, then bought a small weekly paper in Bicknell, Indiana, and served as its editor and publisher. Ten years later the family acquired its flagship paper,

Bill Erickson of The Davis Enterprise *production crew checks a page from the 10-unit press, the largest in Yolo County. The* Enterprise *prints several other newspapers in addition to its own regular and special editions.*

members of the current generations were born. It was founded in 1897 as *The Davisville Enterprise* by L.A. Eichler, and less than six months later Eichler expanded it from a four-page weekly to eight pages. He owned his newspaper only three years, then William H. Scott, a Yolo County native and local justice of the peace, bought it in 1900 and continued as editor and publisher until 1935.

In 1906, soon after Davisville was chosen as the site of the University Farm, Scott dropped the "ville" from the masthead. Perhaps he knew the Davisville Post Office was planning to shorten its name to "Davis," which it did in 1907. Like many newspapers of his day, Scott's *Enterprise* lacked the objectivity expected of newspapers today. In 1906 a front-page headline

Pasting up the newspaper are, from left, compositors Nancy Corstorphine and Anne O'Donnell, and composing room supervisor Leslie Westergaard.

proclaimed: "School Tax Election This Afternoon: Everybody Interested in the Welfare of the Town and School Should Come Out and Vote Tax 'YES.'"

The "Personal and Local Happenings" column on the front page chronicled residents' comings and goings, and told who had been at whose tea party. If you hadn't been invited, you could read it and weep.

Chelso Maghetti, who had come to Davis in 1919, serving as postmaster from 1927 to 1936, bought *The*

Davis Enterprise from Scott in 1935 and published it until 1960.

Three years after Maghetti took over the *Enterprise* won an award from the California Newspaper Publishers Association. Maghetti also made a major contribution to the community by preserving the only complete file of *The Davis Enterprise* in the University of California at Davis Library.

In the 1960s the *Enterprise* became an afternoon newspaper published five days a week, and grew to a circulation of about 1,300 under several different owners. (In 1987 circulation was over 10,000.)

After the McNaughton family purchased the newspaper from the Tibbitts family in March 1967, they built a new office and press building at 302 G Street. The newspaper continued to grow under publisher Phil G. Hays III.

Meanwhile Foy McNaughton, one of Dean McNaughton's two sons, had been serving a seven-year apprenticeship in many facets of newspaper production, including composing, press, circulation, bookkeeping, and advertising. He is now the publisher of *The Davis Enterprise* and chief executive officer of all three McNaughton newspapers in California.

Burt McNaughton, a partner in McNaughton Newspapers, became an advertising sales representative in 1981, and currently is general manager of the *Enterprise* and vice-president of McNaughton Newspapers. Both brothers and their families live in Davis where they are active in community affairs.

Most Enterprise *departments moved to the newly renovated, 8,000-square-foot former post office in 1982. At right, sports editor Tim Oglesby consults with managing editor Debbie Davis. Opposite Davis are news editor Jeff Aberbach and reporter Joel Davis (background).*

In recent years the newspaper has been a consistent top winner in the California Newspaper Publishers Association's annual competitions, as well as in other newspaper contests, winning more than 50 awards since 1980.

The *Enterprise* underwent a major expansion in 1983 with its move to an 8,000-square-foot building at 315 G Street, former site of the post office. Additional expansion will include enlarging the press facility, which is still located in the original plant built by the McNaughtons.

The 10-unit press is the largest in Yolo County and runs night and day as the press crew prints at least three other newspapers in addition to the *Enterprise,* and does many other printing jobs as well.

A 1986 addition to the editorial and classified ad departments is a C-Text computer system, which offers many new options for the staff. But more important than any physical expansion, says Foy McNaughton, is the pledge that "We will continue to own and operate *The Davis Enterprise* in an atmosphere where most family-owned newspapers have been sold to large chains.

"As Davis grows, our philosophy of a community newspaper will not change. We are committed to providing community news first, above all else, and we will stay committed to that goal."

HARRISON REAL ESTATE, INC.

A strong interest in the Davis community and in planning for its future led Sam Harrison, founder of Harrison Real Estate, Inc., to give up management of the then-new G Street Safeway store in Davis, earn a real estate license in 1966, and join Brinley Real Estate Inc. as a salesman, with the goal of establishing his own firm.

Arriving in Davis in 1960, Harrison had served on the Davis Planning Commission from 1964 through 1967, becoming aware of the pressure on developers to produce new housing for a population that had doubled over those four years—from 12,000 to 18,000. Harrison and others saw the need for development under a master plan that would provide for carefully conceived neighborhoods with parks, schools, shopping, and a variety of housing options.

In 1969 he started Harrison Real Estate, opening his first office in Covell Park, one of several such neighborhoods planned for the former Covell tract of some 640 acres north of Covell Boulevard. As exclusive sales agent for Covell Park, Harrison worked in conjunction with two other independent specialists, John Whitcombe of Whitcombe Construction Company and Bill Liggett of Covell Development Company, to develop the area.

While continuing in this informal partnership through 1971, Harrison also had opened a downtown office at 217 E Street in 1970. Since 1972 Harrison and his sales staff, which has included his wife Gwen, two sons, and a daughter, have occupied the former Bank of America building at Second and F streets. Two other children, twins, are completing their educations.

Harrison is proud of his association with Covell Park and earlier with the Stonegate development on the west side of Davis. The north Davis area pioneered the greenbelt concept locally, leading the city to later require greenbelts in all other new developments. Stonegate's homes surround a man-made lake large enough for sailing.

In recent years Harrison Real Estate has diversified with development of buildings for light industry and research, along with general real estate sales. Sam Harrison focuses on developing interior space for tenants through his Harrison Construction and Development Company, managed by son Steve Harrison.

Sam Harrison's community and professional involvement, begun when he first arrived in Davis, has included his holding top offices in the chamber of commerce, Yolo County Board of Realtors, and the Davis Owners and Managers Association; service with the California Association of Realtors, the public schools Curriculum Council, Rotary Club, United Crusade, and Tri-County Planning Council; help in developing a senior high school Work Experience program; and chairmanship of successful county presidential and gubernatorial campaigns for Ronald Reagan and George Deukmejian.

Sam Harrison (left), founder of Harrison Real Estate, and his son Tim, office manager, survey the Covell Park area that Harrison Real Estate, Inc., helped develop. Covell Park pioneered greenbelts in Davis, now required in all new developments.

Harrison Real Estate moved to the former Bank of America building at Second and F streets in 1972. Family members with real estate licenses include Sam, Gwen, Tim, and Steve Harrison and Diana Harrison Bunfill. Twins Jeff and Angie are in college.

SUTTER DAVIS HOSPITAL

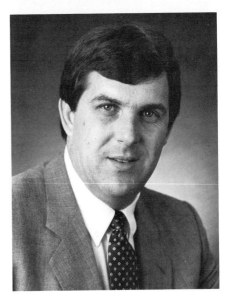

Local autonomy and community pride are important factors in the desire of Sutter Davis Hospital, located just west of Davis, to continually improve current services and add new ones, satisfying a community that expects the best.

The 48-bed acute care facility is part of Sutter Health, a large network of acute and nonacute facilities throughout the West. While enjoying the benefits of efficient management, economic stability, and depth of resources provided by a large medical network, Sutter Davis Hospital remains autonomous, run by a local, active board of trustees and initiating its own special services and programs directly benefiting the local community.

The hospital serves patients from Davis, Dixon, Winters, and Woodland, and its medical staff of 120—including physicians in many specialties, dentists, and podiatrists—is drawn from these areas.

Under previous ownership the institution did not always have the

image of quality care, superior facilities, innovative programs, and community involvement it enjoys today. The hospital was built in 1964 as part of a speculative land development venture that in time went bankrupt. The facility stood empty for almost four years, then was acquired by a private individual and reopened in 1968 as a for-profit hospital. This owner sold it in 1975 to a proprietary hospital chain. When Sutter Community Hospitals purchased it in 1981, Sutter Davis became, for the first time, a not-for-profit community hospital.

Since then the facility's image has been considerably enhanced by a top-notch physician, nursing, and medical-technology staff and an active volunteer auxiliary; a warm and caring approach to patients; cheerful, reassuring surroundings; and many new state-of-the-art technological services previously not available in Davis.

Sutter Davis Hospital does not attempt to duplicate all the ancillary services of larger hospitals, but enjoys excellent cooperation with such institutions and often transfers patients by ambulance, or by helicopter in cases of emergency, for special services.

With the involvement of Sutter Health, the Davis hospital has actively sought community input for the first time in its history, and through concentrated community outreach

Patrick R. Brady, administrator of Sutter Davis Hospital.

with educational programs and special services, it has encouraged personal involvement of local residents in the hospital's future.

Staff members volunteer at community health-screening programs and dispense information at the Davis Senior Center, Dixon May Fair, Winters Youth Day, and the Davis Fourth of July celebration. The annual Sutter Shuffle Fun Run aids patients in the cardiac rehabilitation department's program, and the I Can Cope program sponsors a peer support group for cancer victims and their families. A new monthly guest weekend program—the first of its kind in a California acute care hospital—offers care and activities to persons requiring 24-hour supervision, giving their family caregivers a weekend of respite.

"We may have one of the most innovative small hospitals in the state of California," says Sutter Davis administrator Patrick Brady.

INSET: Medical staff orthopedic surgeon William W. Winternitz, Jr., M.D., performs arthroscopic surgery in one of the two Sutter Davis Hospital operating rooms assisted by operating room nurse Pat Horner, R.N., and anesthesiologist Jack Rosenberg, M.D., while the patient watches the view of her knee on the TV monitor.

RIGHT: A helicopter team prepares to take a critically injured patient to the Sacramento Medical Center of the University of California, Davis, Medical Center. Assisting the patient are Dr. Charles Keller (left), technician Mike Hinman, and emergency department nurse Sara Doneen, R.N.

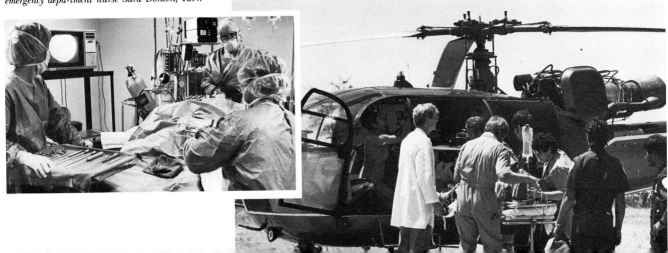

CRANSTON BROTHERS ACE HARDWARE

Cranston Brothers Ace Hardware of Woodland has always been a family business—and the store's employees have always felt like family, too. "They never leave," jokes Eldon Cranston, current owner/manager with his wife, Nancy.

Homer Cook, an all-around hardware person, has been with the company 51 years. Another employee came to help out during an illness and stayed 33 years, and many of the 19 employees have been there 30 to 35 years.

Perhaps employees feel comfort-

able at Cranston's because the store itself hasn't changed much since it was built in 1914 by Eldon Cranston's grandfather, Reuben Borton "R.B." Cranston. He established his first store in 1898. R.B. Cranston had driven for a Woodland-Capay Valley stagecoach line before working several years for a local hardware company, and then opening his own small store. He outgrew it quickly and moved a few doors away to a larger building on the corner of First and Main streets.

When he built the current Cranston's at 618 Main Street, R.B. was joined by his three sons, Lester, George, and Thornton. The store featured a drinking fountain out front, for the convenience of customers and passersby. The City of Woodland apparently appreciated this amenity for the citizenry of a hot climate, because it paid to have a large block of ice delivered daily, to cool the fountain. The fountain remains, but these days the water is electrically refrigerated.

After R.B. Cranston died in 1922, his sons continued in the business, enlarging and remodeling the store but keeping the old-fashioned look and atmosphere still to be found there. A mezzanine runs around three sides of the long, narrow room, and shelves

Reuben Borton Cranston, founder of R.B. Cranston Hardware.

upstairs and down are jammed with high-quality, practical items. Little attention is given to frills, but a lot is given to service.

Eldon Cranston says townspeople often bring visitors downtown to see what a hardware store of yesteryear looked like. Cranston's also serves as a casual meeting place. "It's like the old general store," he remarks, "but without the groceries and variety items." One secret for keeping track of all the merchandise is to stock what people want, and eliminate items that don't move well.

Nancy Cranston has given a more modern, artistic look to her area of quality housewares and gifts in an adjoining but separate section.

Eldon, son of George Cranston, joined the business in 1947 after leaving the armed forces. There was a partnership of seven family members at that time; but on April 1, 1965, Eldon and Nancy Cranston bought out the last partner.

Both Cranstons have been active in community affairs, but these days are just concentrating on keeping the store the way Woodlanders expect it to be. "We're closed only six days of the year," says Eldon. "Our emphasis has always been on service."

Cranston Hardware has occupied three sites since its founding in 1898. This building, erected by R.B. Cranston in 1914, is a Main Street landmark and still houses the thriving Cranston Brothers Ace Hardware.

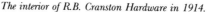

The interior of R.B. Cranston Hardware in 1914.

WELLS FARGO BANK

Wells Fargo & Company was organized in New York City in March 1852 by Henry Wells, William G. Fargo, and some of their associates, specifically to operate in California's burgeoning goldfields. A joint express and banking office opened in San Francisco on July 13 of that year, and a branch opened in Sacramento at the same time. Those were the first of some 10,000 offices eventually serving the nation by 1918.

Wells Fargo's first presence in Yolo County was in Cacheville (now Yolo) and Knights Landing in 1861, operating through locally appointed agents. F.S. Freeman became agent in Woodland in 1863. The firm opened its own office on Main Street in 1873.

By the end of the 1870s Wells Fargo & Company also was represented in Blacks (now Zamora), Cache Creek (later Madison), Clarksburg, Davisville, Dunnigan, and Winters.

In 1905 the organization's banking functions, which had been conducted under the style of Wells Fargo & Co.'s Bank, were completely separated from the express functions. The latter ceased in 1918, when the federal government consolidated the nation's domestic express operations into the American Railway Express Company.

Yolo County's first bank, the Bank of Woodland (not related to the present Bank of Woodland), opened for business in February 1869. Its first location was at the present site of Woody's Jewelry on Main Street, near First Street. In 1873 the institution moved into newly refurbished quarters on the southwest corner of Main and First streets, where it conducted business for more than 40 years.

Another bank, the Yolo County Savings Bank, commenced business in 1892 and built the gray limestone building still located at Main and College streets. That structure was remodeled in 1914 to make room for the Bank of Woodland, with the two businesses operating separately but in the same premises.

Both of these institutions were purchased in March 1950 by the American Trust Company, which 10 years later merged with Wells Fargo Bank and assumed the latter's name. In 1963 the organization moved to its present location at Court and College streets.

Crocker Citizens National Bank, which traces its origins back to 1870 in San Francisco, opened an office in Woodland in September 1966. Wells Fargo acquired Crocker in May 1986, and the two Woodland offices were consolidated under the Wells Fargo

After the Gold Rush inspired formation of the Wells Fargo express and banking company, the Wells Fargo wagon became the most reliable method of carrying gold for assay, mail, and necessary goods to residents of remote areas.

name. This office has the largest total deposits of any bank in Yolo County, as had its predecessors for the past 118 years.

Wells Fargo Bank opened its office in Davis in May 1963. A West Sacramento office opened in July 1964, but was closed in January 1985. Wells Fargo returned to the West Sacramento community with the Crocker acquisition in mid-1986.

Wells Fargo Bank has three separate offices in the Yolo County area; they are (from left) the Davis office, the West Sacramento office, and the Woodland office (right).

PACIFIC INTERNATIONAL RICE MILLS, INC.

Yolo County has long been known as a place where rice will grow easily. What may not be commonly recognized is the way local rice production and export are influenced by the fortunes of other parts of the world. Wars and other political factors affecting Japan, Korea, and Vietnam—all rice-growing and rice-consuming nations—have at different times put the United States in the position of exporting rice to these countries.

In fact, says Curt M. Rocca of Woodland, founder and president from 1953 to 1982 of Pacific International Rice Mills, Inc., of Woodland—informally known as PIRMI—the United States is second only to Thailand in the exporting of rice. Yet this country grows just over 2 percent of the world's total product. Says Walt Ramazzini, general manager of PIRMI, one must realize that Americans can produce rice far in excess of what they will consume. In the Asian countries, where rice dominates the daily diet, the grain has often had to be imported to satisfy the need, especially when family and

commercial production had given way to a war effort.

Currently, since such countries have increasingly recovered their ability to produce, PIRMI ships mainly to European countries, and also has found a substantial market in the Asian communities in this country. Among the varieties helping satisfy the latter market is sweet rice, a glutenous

Gordon Kliewer, right, who is still with PIRMI in 1987, was filling bags of Extra Fancy Kokeshi Rice for the Asian market in the early 1960s.

rice used by Asians for confectionary dishes and fortune cookies.

As the needs of world populations have shifted, so have the facilities of PIRMI, which started in Woodland and is still based there. Over the years the company has acquired or built mills and other plants at locations around the world, then sold them off as the need for those particular facilities ceased to exist because local rice growers had become active once more.

Pacific International Rice Mills, Inc., was established as a corporation in San Francisco in 1953. Reincorporating in 1954, PIRMI acquired the Stockton Elevator Company and built a grain terminal in Stockton for the export of bulk rice. Since the Port of Sacramento had not yet been established, the first exporting of rice was done from Stockton in 1959.

Soon the company was exporting not only rice, but barley, wheat, and corn, and was the largest grain complex in California. That same year the company leased the facilities of the Producers Rice Milling Company, owned by Ernie Brown of Woodland.

In 1962 the firm, under Rocca's leadership, bought the Sunset Rice Dryer in Woodland from Woodlander

Construction began in 1962 on the Pacific International Rice Mills, Inc. (PIRMI), plant in Woodland, at the site of the Sunset Rice Dryer. Sunset's drying and storage facilities were expanded at the same time.

The ANNA C., a newly converted bulk rice carrier, was being loaded with its first shipment of premium rice in a new Okinawan service from the Port of Stockton, inaugurated in 1959 by PIRMI of Woodland.

Officers and directors of Central Valley Rice Growers posing aboard the ANNA C. are, from left, Ross Lyon, treasurer, Maxwell; Orvil Geer, director, Woodland; Tom Butler, vice-president, Woodland; Jack Carrico, director, Woodland; Bill Geer, president, Woodland; and Sam Shannon, secretary, Yuba City.

Regner Paulson, and that year started construction of the present rice mill on the Sunset property at Kentucky Avenue and East Street, also expanding Sunset's drying and storage facilities.

Rocca and the other stockholders owned the company until 1982, when they sold it to Jack Anderson and Jack Wallace of Yolo County. The new owners sold the operation to the Rice Growers Association of California in 1984. Then a successful antitrust suit brought against RGA forced the sale of the Woodland facility, and it was purchased on August 15, 1986, by the present owners, Busch Agricultural Resources, Inc., a wholly owned subsidiary of Anheuser-Busch.

Over the years PIRMI acquired additional drying and storage facilities at Robbins and at the Dettling Farms north of Woodland. Among other acquisitions or new construction of the company, purchased to fill a particular need at the time, were the Pacific Rice Company of Okinawa, then still U.S.-occupied (1964); and the Okinawa Food Company, the largest miller of rice in the southern Japanese islands (1966).

In 1973 PIRMI founded the Korea Silo Company in Inchon, Korea, to handle bulk rice and grains, and in 1974 founded the Taehan Bulk Silo Company in Inchon, the largest grain silo complex in the Far East.

In 1977-1978 PIRMI built PIRMI Delta Inc., a large rice drying and milling complex at Greenville, Mississippi, on the Mississippi River. The company also acquired, in conjunction with Nomura and Co. of San Francisco, Rice Research, Inc., at Bayless, California, in order to develop new strains and perfect the premium rices already being sold. The latter includes Kukoho Rose, the number-one preferred rice of the Japanese and Korean communities in the United States.

In 1978 PIRMI acquired the majority stock of Agricom International, with an oil seed extraction plant at Grimes, California, and a refinery in Berkeley. That same year PIRMI started and built the Numano Saki Co. in Berkeley, the first saki plant in the United States. In 1965 PIRMI had sold part of the Kentucky Avenue property to Pacific Oil Seeds, a sister company. This facility exists for the promotion and development of pure bred safflower and other oil seed crops, such as sunflower and sesame.

PIRMI opened an office in Japan during a period of heavy exportation to that country between 1968 and 1983. In 1981 the sales of PIRMI and its affiliates were approximately $400 million. After years of exportation to Japan and Korea, the chief market for PIRMI now is Europe, although the firm ships to almost every country in the world. Consumption of rice also is increasing in the United States.

PIRMI, having now divested itself of most of its affiliate companies, is proud to have opened up the Far East at a time when there were more people than there was rice to feed

Ray Kipker sets rice whiteners in the PIRMI plant during the late 1960s.

Gordon Kliewer sews shut the tops of bags of rice in PIRMI's Woodland mill during the 1960s. The rice was destined for the Orient at a time when growers there hadn't been able to produce enough to feed their countrymen.

them. PIRMI has also increased exports to European markets, and pioneered the bulk shipment of rice.

California producers shipped the first seed rice to Australia, and both the private and government sectors have sent advisors to countries starting rice production.

In addition to producing bulk rice for export, PIRMI makes and packages a number of rice products for domestic consumption. They include U.S. No. 1, 4-percent premium white rice, long-grain rice, brown rice, sweet rice, and short-grain rice.

The company sponsored the formation, in 1955, of the Central Valley Rice Growers, a group of Sacramento Valley growers under contract to PIRMI. Phil Larner was the first president of this association.

The PIRMI plant in Woodland can mill about 5 million hundredweights (100-pound units) of paddy rice (rough from the fields) per year. That's a lot of rice.

COLDWELL BANKER DOUG ARNOLD REAL ESTATE, INC.

The Doug Arnold Real Estate Company—now Coldwell Banker Doug Arnold Real Estate, Inc.—was actually started by Bill Arnold, who showed the Davis and Yolo County community that if one enjoys working with people and truly believes in his product he can be successful at selling anything.

Following in the footsteps of his father, Horace Douglas Arnold, Bill Arnold was an automobile dealer before going into real estate. Later Bill's only son, Bill Douglas Arnold, Jr., would join him in real estate; he is president of the company today. No one, however, continued in the latter profession of Horace "H.D." Arnold; after he left his automobile dealership he opened a furniture and appliance store.

Almost the entire history of the Arnold-Erway-Brown families is rooted in the Yolo County and Sacramento areas. Bill Arnold's parents met in Broderick, where their families' backyards adjoined. Both families had come from England.

Although neighbors, H.D. Arnold and Lillian Erway really first noticed each other in 1902, and were married

This building at 975 Olive Drive, the home of Arnold Motor Co. in Davis from 1962 until 1967, now houses another business, but the original Arnold Motor Co. building at the corner of First and F streets is gone.

seven years later. Then they moved across the river to Sacramento, where H.D. and his brother J.H. "Harry" Arnold had opened that city's first automobile dealership in 1906, later to be known as the founders of Sacramento's Automobile Row. The H.D. Arnolds' two sons were Horace Jr. and Bill (like his son, never "William").

The young woman Bill later married, Nanele Brown, also was a native Californian with ties to Yolo County; so were her mother and maternal grandparents. Nanele was the daughter of Fred "Fritz" Brown, a charter member of Alpha Gamma Rho fraternity at the University of California at Davis (then University Farm), from which he graduated in 1922, becoming president of the alumni association in 1925.

The family can't substantiate the claim of Nanele's late mother, Audrey Brown, that she was "Queen of the Causeway" at the opening celebration of the Yolo Causeway. But Nanele doesn't doubt her mother's memories of the pre-causeway era, when one couldn't drive to Sacramento from Davis during the winter floods. The choices were the train or driving around by way of Stockton. Even after the causeway was in, says Bill Arnold, driving to Sacramento from Davis was difficult on the two-lane road with a white line down the middle. There

Horace "H.D." Arnold (left), father of Bill D. Arnold and grandfather of B. Douglas Arnold, poses with his brother Harry at their car dealership at the corner of 18th Street and Capitol Avenue in Sacramento. The car is a new 1934 Buick.

were no cloverleaf approaches to the highway, and crossing against the traffic to go east was extremely difficult.

Things improved when a new causeway was completed in the 1960s, south of the old one that had been built of redwood and had barrels of water every 200 feet in case of fire. In the huge floods of 1955, the old causeway had to be sandbagged.

Bill and Nanele lived in Sacramento, but moved to Davis when their son Doug was six years old. H.D. Arnold's company had mostly dealt with Hudson and Essex cars; but in June 1955 Bill started a Pontiac dealership in Davis, continuing in the automobile business until 1967. The business was at First and F streets, moving later to a new building completed in 1962 at 975 Olive Drive.

These were convenient locations; the dealership had easy access to the railroad station and an adjoining loading dock, so the Arnold Motor

At present the Arnold offices are in the old Hamel residence, built by the son of early pioneers who ranched just south of Davisville in Solano County. The house is listed in the Historic Resources Survey of Yolo County.

From left are Nanele F. Arnold, Bill D. Arnold, B. Douglas Arnold, and Donna J. Arnold, at the wedding of Doug and Donna Arnold on February 14, 1987.

Company won the contract to provide the last servicing for all the new Pontiacs before they were delivered to the California Highway Patrol in 1957.

The company got $25 per car; for this it did a $1.95 lube job, made sure everything worked, and cleaned the automobile, usually dusty from the freight cars, until it was spic and span. Then Arnold would hire students from the Delta Sigma Phi fraternity house (at the future Larry Blake's-Brewster House location) to drive the cars to Sacramento. "But because there was no place to put a lot of cars in downtown Sacramento," says Bill, "they'd be parked all over Davis until the Highway Patrol was ready for them."

Bill Arnold had been "dabbling in real estate here and there" for several years, and finally opened a real estate business in 1973 at 122 B Street in Davis. Doug Arnold left his job as a San Francisco policeman to join his father the following year.

The company moved briefly to 123 D Street, and then to the present office in the former H.J. Hamel residence at 505 Second Street, built in 1920 by Henry J. and Lida Hamel. Henry was the son of an early ranching family from just south of Davisville in Solano County. The house, which the Arnolds have filled with period furnishings, combines Colonial Revival and Craftsman architectural elements and is notable for an unusual second-story bay window.

In 1975 Arnold Real Estate opened a Woodland office, has since had branches in Winters and West Sacramento, and currently has offices in Woodland and Dixon.

Bill turned the company over to Doug a few years ago, but both he and Nanele stay active in real estate sales, as does Doug's wife, Donna.

In 1985 Doug Arnold Real Estate affiliated with Coldwell Banker, a member of the Sears Financial Network and the nation's largest full-service real estate company. In 1987 Coldwell Banker Doug Arnold Real Estate, Inc., was moved into the prestigious Chairman's Circle, in recognition of the new affiliate's "entrepreneurial drive and excellent performance" in 1986. The Arnold operation was one of 42 chosen by the 80-year-old Coldwell Banker organization out of some 900 affiliates.

The Arnolds, who continue to own and operate the agency, believe their business has been so successful because "we hire people who are really serious about real estate, and about serving people.

"In our family we've been salespeople for 80 years. All of our agents are local people who've been here a long time, and who care about the community." Doug Arnold recalls that recently, when the real estate board's Davis Division chairman asked for volunteers for an important community effort, eight people raised their hands and six of these were from Arnold's.

All the Arnolds have been active in community affairs. Serving in different years, Bill has been president and Doug the secretary/treasurer of the Yolo County Board of Realtors; both have been named Realtor of the Year, and both have served as president of the Davis Chamber of Commerce. Father and son are active in Davis Rotary, and Doug Arnold is chairman of the Yolo County Housing Authority.

THE ELECTRIC GARAGE CO.

That a Woodland dealership selling and servicing the very latest in gasoline-powered automobiles should be called The Electric Garage Co. may seem odd. But there is a very good reason for the name. Back in 1909, when the business was founded by the current owner's grandfather, electric cars were what most people were driving—if indeed they had a car at all.

Gasoline automobile engines were just being developed around 1904 or 1905, and people hadn't quite made up their minds about them yet. On the other hand people were accustomed to electric trolley cars, and the first "horseless carriages" were electrics.

When something went wrong with some part of the electrical system in those cars, Woodland people would arrive at the home of William Dahler, chief lineman for Pacific Telephone and a recognized whiz at electrical and machine work, asking for his help. "They'd pull up in front of the house on weekends," his grandson, R.M. "Lonny" Pritchard, says, "and ask him to come out on the lawn and look at their cars."

As Dahler solved people's automotive problems on his front lawn and in his spare time, his reputation grew. Finally he decided to open an electric service shop at the corner of Main and Third streets, in a small brick building owned by the Woodland Odd Fellows. Dahler and a partner put up a sign reading "Electric Garage" and quietly told a few friends they would do automobile electrical work, wash cars, scrub brass, and perform other small jobs.

At that time electric car manufacturers didn't even make lights for their cars—if people drove at night they carried gas lights. Soon The Electric Garage Co. had built a large business of installing electrical lighting systems.

"There was no such thing as a service station then," says current owner Lonny Pritchard. "There was no name for a car dealer, either—but just the common terminologies of 'livery stable' and 'garage'." "Livery stable" didn't fit, but "garage" did, especially after some of the automobile manufacturers started approaching Dahler, asking him to carry a few of their cars. The first car the company took on was Studebaker's E.M.F.

Electric Garage founder William Dahler, shown in his later years, much preferred being a "grease monkey" to taking care of business matters. He left that to his son-in-law Morris A. Pritchard, who enjoyed meeting the public.

model, an electric.

The Studebakers had been wagon makers since 1852; their expertise was in the building of coaches, so it made sense 50 years later to add electric motors to the vehicle bodies they were building. Moving with the times, the Studebaker company became one of the largest manufacturers of electric cars, and later made a smooth transition to internal combustion engines.

In just 10 years the dealership/service garage started by Dahler and called The Electric Garage Co. had become one of the largest in existence anywhere in the country. Dahler was

R.L. "Lonny" Pritchard, current owner and the third-generation member in a four-generation family of owner/staff persons in The Electric Garage Co., stands by some of the original doors in the building occupied by the company since 1910.

the repairman, and hired someone else to manage the business end. In 1936 he brought in his son-in-law, Morris A. Pritchard, to run the business, and much later they were joined by Pritchard's only son, Lonny.

"The son worked in the back with his grandfather, with grease on his hands," says Lonny Pritchard of himself, "while his father was up front." Morris Pritchard was an extrovert who enjoyed involvement with people and the community, while his father-in-law much preferred working with his hands behind the scenes.

Even after Lonny moved up front to take over the business end of the enterprise in 1976, owing to his father's advancing age, Morris was really the boss, he says. Morris Pritchard died in March 1982, the day before he was to turn 80. His widow, Dorothy, still lives in the home the family built on Second Street in Woodland.

William Dahler had died in 1948,

and the Pritchards had bought out other family members to become sole owners of The Electric Garage Co. Now Lonny Pritchard oversees both the business and the service end of the large company, in a huge building that was expanded in 1912 and has been remodeled and refurbished several times since then.

After only 18 months in business The Electric Garage Co. had moved to a much larger building facing on Main Street, and the plant has continued to expand at frequent intervals while still occupying the same site. In time the building came to contain a large automobile sales and display room, a parts department,

and electrical, battery, and tire shops, as well as a larger mechanical department. As early as 1920 it was already being said that the garage and its owner had the capacity to turn out an entire automobile, or even a tractor, should these be called for. The firm had one of the largest stocks of parts in the Sacramento Valley, and met the largest monthly payroll in Yolo County.

In 1987 the fourth generation in The Electric Garage Co. includes Lonny Pritchard's son Stephen, who will soon graduate from high school

This license plate card on a new four-wheel-drive vehicle in the showroom speaks for itself.

and who works in the service department after school, and his daughter Dorothy, who has worked in the office and is now a college student.

Today The Electric Garage Co. is equipped to do any kind of automotive repair work, and has 25 full- and part-time employees. After dealing in various makes of vehicles over the years, including Cadillac, National, and Maxwell cars; Yuba Ball Tread and Fageol tractors; Federal and Maxwell trucks; and Utility trailers, the firm now has the Woodland franchise for Chrysler, Dodge, and Plymouth automobiles and Dodge trucks.

While times have changed, and William Dahler is no longer there to turn out machine work for farmers by hand as he once did, the old-fashioned personal service he offered back in 1909 is still a point of pride with those who operate and work at The Electric Garage Co.

The Electric Garage Co. moved around the corner to this building shortly after its 1909 founding to accommodate increasing business. The top of the facade, formerly brick, has been replaced by wood, but the bricks below are the original ones.

RALEY'S

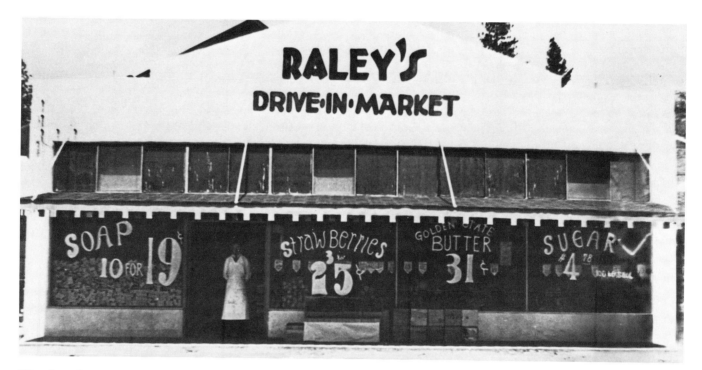

West has always been the direction of destiny for Thomas P. Raley, whose billion-dollar supermarket and drug center chain is headquartered at 500 West Capitol Avenue in West Sacramento. Born in 1903, the 13th child of a rural Baptist preacher and farmer, Raley could have stayed in his native state of Arkansas and also become a farmer. Instead, he headed out to California in the early 1920s in search of his fortune. He found it.

Raley settled first in Los Angeles, where he worked as a delivery man for a bottled water company. Noting, as he delivered his products in the pouring rain, that his customers did their work indoors, he made a quick change of career direction. A call to the Safeway Markets office put him in touch with the vice-president, who put Raley to work. After managing a couple of Safeway Markets, Raley decided to try his luck as a store owner.

A recommendation from Safeway's founder, M.B. Skaggs, enabled him to open his first store on Main Street in Placerville. On opening day Raley put his own total savings of $125 into the till to make change. He advertised his establishment as the "first drive-in market." He had one employee, Cleo Seals.

This tiny 2,500-square-foot market was the seed from which blossomed the present Raley empire of 51 superstores (a marketing concept pioneered by Raley), 6,500 employees, and a payroll in excess of $117 million.

Twenty-five years ago Raley made another move west—this time across the Sacramento River to what was then Broderick (now part of the new city of West Sacramento, incorporated January 1, 1987). Sensing the potential for growth in the small community, with its corridor of motels and small businesses, Raley began buying property. He eventually acquired 20 acres along and near the riverfront.

"Four or five guys were putting up a motel by the river," he recalls. "One of them approached me and wanted to sell out his share. Later on I bought them all out and finished the building." That was the Marina Inn, for many years a popular riverfront motel, conference center, supper club, and docking area for boaters. The Marina Inn was closed officially in 1986 to

Anyone today would be happy to pay the prices charged at Raley's first store in Placerville, advertised as a "Drive-In Market" by the innovative founder of a chain of "superstores" now numbering 51.

make room for a new $150-million development along the river, which included a marina, hotel, and other commercial ventures.

In 1984 Raley's Corporation moved from offices occupied for 25 years at 1515 20th Street in Sacramento into the 65,000-square-foot Corporate Center on West Capitol Avenue. A few blocks up the street is a Raley's Superstore, where shoppers can pick up tickets for a Caribbean cruise or purchase insurance at the same time they buy carrots and cough drops.

An older store at 940 Sacramento Avenue, in what was then Broderick, closed in the fall of 1984 when the West Capitol Avenue Market opened. The historic older store was the first of Raley's supermarket-drugstore operations. His idea was that customers would appreciate being able to make only one stop for their grocery, drug, and variety needs. A 50-percent increase in sales in both departments proved he was correct.

Several years later the wall separating the two sections was removed in most of the older stores, and eliminated completely in new construction. It was the birth of the superstore. Raley's giant 60,000-square-feet-plus stores now hold not only drug and grocery items, but full-service delicatessens and bakeries, as well as separate travel centers and insurance sales islands.

"I'm a part of Yolo County," Raley says. "I like being here." A new superstore opened in May 1987 on Main Street in Woodland. It is one of the largest in the chain, and replaces the tiny store at 1349 College Street, where Woodlanders have shopped for more than 30 years. Raley's officials hope to one day see one of their superstores in Davis also.

Raley's is a family affair. Raley is sole owner and chairman of the company. His only daughter, Joyce Raley Teel, is director of employee and community relations. Her husband, James E. Teel, is vice-president of operations. Teel's brother, Robert, is director of drug operations. Raley's president, Charles L. Collings, and his brother, Kenneth H. Collings,

Thomas P. Raley came in out of the rain some 60 years ago to enter the grocery business and introduce a new concept in marketing that puts food, drugs, variety items, and even travel and insurance services under one roof.

hired into the company within two years of one another.

Throughout its history, Raley's has found many of its key personnel among people who had family members already working for the firm. The employee roster lists numerous families where husbands, wives, and children are employed in different stores or departments.

Joyce Teel grew up in the business and remembers playing in the back room of one of her father's stores as he worked. She washed meat bins and used a flatiron to seal meat packages in the days before the machinery to do this had been invented. Her four daughters and one son all have worked for the company, and the Teel sons-in-law also are employed in the family business.

Perhaps because of its strong family orientation, Raley's has an outstanding record of corporate community involvement. The Christmas 1986 Food for Families, done with KCRA Channel 3 TV, collected 10 semitrucks worth of donated food. The company further committed $50,000 for perishable goods. The food was distributed to food closets in all California and Nevada communities where Raley's stores are located.

An anti-drug abuse program was conducted in the stores. CPR Saturday, cosponsored by the American Red Cross and teaching cardiopulmonary resuscitation, is in its second

year. In another health-related campaign, Raley's Melt-A-Million Pounds Rotation Diet drew 162,000 participants. A spring promotion encouraging regular mammograms is planned. Joyce Teel also writes a column titled "Caring" for the company in-house magazine. In it recognition is given to individual employees who donate outstanding community service.

Raley's also has been a generous supporter of the Sacramento Symphony and the Crocker Art Museum of Sacramento. The West Sacramento Corporate Center is frequently toured by art lovers to view its extensive collection of wall art and sculpture.

"Tom" Raley's personal business philosophy was expressed in a *Sacramento Union* business profile a few years ago. "Treat others the way you would like to be treated. You feel good when you've treated people right. Then they come back and do the same for you."

The corporate headquarters in West Sacramento for Raley's supermarkets and drug centers provides offices for many family members and other longtime employees. Collectively, Raley's executives and employees have a tradition of community service involvement.

BRINLEY'S REAL ESTATE INC.

The house where Brinley's Real Estate is located was, many years before, the home of John and Laurette Brinley and their young children, and earlier still, the home of Dr. Walter E. Bates, Davis' first physician.

The Brinleys, who started Brinley's Real Estate Inc., have a long history, and so does the house in which the agency is located. The building at 401 Second Street in Davis was originally owned by Davis' first physician, Dr. Walter E. Bates, and later purchased by John and Laurette Brinley as a home for their young family. Many years later the Brinleys reclaimed the charming house and made it the fourth of the company's offices.

Started by John Brinley's father, A.G. "Sam" Brinley, in 1947, Brinley's was located first on G Street; next at 711 Second Street, Dr. Leo Cronan's former office; and then at 204 E Street, in the Brinley Building, before moving to its present location in April 1979.

Sam Brinley retired early from his job as Southern Pacific agent to start his real estate business, the third in Davis after those of Ben French and J.W. Long. Today Brinley's is the oldest continuing firm in Davis. John Brinley, who'd been with the Bank of Davis, joined his father and one secretary, Mrs. McWalters, in 1949. Over the next 35 years Sam and John Brinley learned to adapt to changes as a "very small and very quiet town" mushroomed along with a rapidly growing campus.

Although Sam was prominent in the community until his death in 1961,

Sam Brinley, active in community affairs, had always wanted a real estate company, so he retired early from his position as Southern Pacific station agent to found Brinley's, the oldest continuing real estate firm in Davis.

his wife's family were the real pioneers. Sam arrived in 1912, shortly after the university opened. First a telegrapher for the railroad and later the agent, he roomed, as a single man, at the home of George Weber, who started the first saloon in Davis.

Sam married Gertrude Frances Weber and they had two children, Betty Ann and John. But the little girl, not yet two, died in the 1918 influenza epidemic that had hit Davis hard. "Dr. Bates was taking care of the whole

town," John Brinley says.

Sam was "a joiner"—a founder of Rotary Club and the chamber of commerce and an avid Democrat (while remaining registered as a Republican). During World War II Brinley, as station agent, helped recruit townspeople as a section gang to keep the tracks in good repair. High school principal Delmar Marshall, Charles Kaufman, and Merton Love were among those volunteering.

John Brinley's volunteer involvement includes the Yolo County Historical Society, the Library Associates, and the UC Davis Arboretum. He is a former commissioner of the Yolo County Housing Authority.

Owing to a housing shortage, as newlyweds John and Laurette Suez Brinley lived with John's parents, finally buying land on Olive Drive and building a modular prefabricated house—so unconventional some looked upon it with disdain. At one time there was but a single house on the market; real estate firms survived on their insurance businesses. But when University Farm became a full university in 1952, real estate "exploded."

In March 1983 John Brinley retired, offering the business to the agents then on his staff. Management of Brinley's Real Estate Inc. continues under the leadership of Gerald P. Kenny, who is in his 35th year with the firm. Current owners are grateful for Brinley's confidence in them, and Brinley is pleased the firm "is continuing with the same name and the same philosophy, that is that clients—both buyers and sellers—should receive the best service a firm can provide.

"You build your business on building a good name."

THE WEBER FAMILY

"A noble Christian woman went to her reward when on Friday the 10th of January death summoned the gentle spirit of Mrs. Annie Weber to her heavenly home." Mary Ann Hunt Weber and her husband, George Augustus Weber, together had a positive influence on the community that is still felt today.

The 1912 obituary for "Annie" Weber was one of several describing her selflessness in carrying food to the sick, working to establish a Catholic mission parish (priests often stayed at the Weber home), and raising four daughters, all of whom stayed to enhance the community.

Born August 25, 1850, in Kenosha, Wisconsin, Annie came west in 1862 by way of the Isthmus of Panama with her two brothers after their parents died. They settled on farmland south of Old Putah Creek, and Annie was just 12 when she started housekeeping for her older and younger brother while they went to school. At age 19 she married George Weber; their first home was at 223 C Street. Weber, born January 13, 1835, had come overland from Liverpool, Medina County, Ohio, in 1853, with three older brothers. George worked for Jonathan Sikes in the Tremont District, then returned home to serve in the Ohio Regiment in the Civil War.

Returning to Davisville, Weber worked in William Dresbach's store, saving money to open his own saloon—the first in Davis, but later followed by many others, as well as hotels and "a couple of very small grocery stores," according to grandson John Brinley.

The one-room structure was a shed from a stagecoach stop; Weber had it moved opposite the railroad depot about 1875, after purchasing the prime business location from Dresbach for $400 in gold coin. The Yolo Saloon and Billiard Parlor continued as a popular "gentleman's

retreat" even after the selling of alcoholic beverages was prohibited in 1911.

In 1880 George and Annie Weber purchased a large Victorian house at Second and E streets; it was the family residence until it made way for the Brinley Building in 1963.

Two of the couple's four daughters married into pioneer families. Mary Ann (1871-1932) married W. Jeff Montgomery and their daughter, Georgene, married Jack Jackson. Ida Madora (1874-1940) married William Greive, a herdsman at the University Farm for many years and the son of Charles S. and Annie Greive. They had a son, Charles. Ida's nephew John Brinley had a great fondness for "Uncle Bill" Greive, regarding him as "a second father."

Harriet Elisha (1872-1961) was the only unmarried Weber daughter. "Miss Hattie" was librarian of the Davisville Library, then in the Buena Vista Hotel, and later the first librarian of a new Yolo County library,

Members of the George Augustus Weber family gathered for a photograph, probably in the 1890s. The photographer later touched up his print with charcoal. From left are Mary Ann Hunt Weber, Gertrude Frances Weber (Brinley), Ida Madora Weber (Greive), George Augustus Weber, Harriet Elisha Weber, and Mary Ann Weber Montgomery with baby Georgene (later Jackson).

until she retired in 1955.

Gertrude Frances (1885-1961) was the first librarian at the University Farm and later a stenographer and bookkeeper at the farm's creamery department. She married Al Green "Sam" Brinley, who'd been the Southern Pacific agent and later established Brinley's Real Estate and Insurance Office. The Brinley Award, named for Sam, is given each year to an individual for outstanding contributions to community life.

The Brinleys' daughter, Betty Ann, died in 1918 during the influenza epidemic. Their son, John, married Laurette Suez, and the couple has four children.

PATRONS

The following individuals, companies, and organizations have made a valuable commitment to the quality of this publication. Windsor Publications and the Yolo County Historical Society and the Yolo County Superintendent of Schools gratefully acknowledge their participation in *Yolo County: Land of Changing Patterns.*

A-1 Appliance
Abele Farms
Bank of Woodland*
W.J. Blevins Medical Group, Inc.*
Brinley's Real Estate Inc.*
Campus Chevrolet/Toyota
The Carlon Company
Carousel Stationery
Celoni Oil Co.
Herbert W. Chandler, Retired Yolo
    County Agricultural Commissioner
City of Davis, David Rosenberg, Mayor
Coldwell Banker Doug Arnold Real
    Estate, Inc.*
Dr. & Mrs. T.Y. Cooper
Ilse Corbett-Grant
Cranston Brothers Ace Hardware*
Cranston International, Inc.
Davis Chamber of Commerce
The Davis Enterprise*
Davis Joint Unified School District
Davis Lumber & Hardware Company*
Ditch Witch Equipment Co., Inc.
The Electric Garage Co.*
Eleanor Emison
Esparto Unified School District
First Northern Bank*
Joe and Terry Garcia
Geyer Associates
Robert L. Griffith & Associates
Harrison Real Estate, Inc.*
The Milton Lee Family
Mark - Gerda Faye
Millsap, Millsap, and Thompson,
    Attorneys
Pacific International Rice Mills, Inc.*
Pepsi-Cola Bottling Co.

Raley's*
Jane Morris Reiff
Richard & Evelyne Rominger
Mrs. Patricia Chiles Schlabes
Joseph Schwarzgruber & Sons
Virginia Sprague
Spreckels Sugar Company, Inc.
Sutter Davis Hospital*
Richard F. Walters
Washington Unified School District
    August Vieceli, Superintendent
The Weber Family*
Wells Fargo Bank*
Western Title Insurance Company*
West Sacramento Land Company*
Wm. P. Wilson & Son's, Inc.
Woodland Clinic Medical Group*
Woodland Joint Unified School District
Woodland Memorial Hospital*
Woodland Travel
Yolo County Archives-Volunteers in
    Preservation
Yolo County Libraries*

*Partners in Progress of *Yolo County: Land of Changing Patterns.* The histories of these companies and organizations appear in Chapter 8, beginning on page 101.

BIBLIOGRAPHY

BOOKS AND ARTICLES

Bainer, Roy. *The Engineering of Abundance: An Oral History Memoir of Roy Bainer*. Davis: University Library, 1975.

Bancroft, Hubert Howe. *History of California*. Santa Barbara: Wallace Hobbard, 1963-1970.

Becker, Robert H. *Designs on the Land*. San Francisco: Book Club of California, 1969.

——————. *Diseños of California Ranchos*. San Francisco: Book Club of California, 1964.

Blow, Ben. *California Highways*. San Francisco: California State Automobile Association, 1920.

Caughey, John W. *California*. Englewood Cliffs, NJ: Prentice-Hall, 1970.

Clover, Haworth A. *Hesperian College 1861-1896*. Burlingame, CA: The Hesperia Press, 1974.

Cutter, Donald C. "Spanish Exploration of California's Central Valley." Unpublished Ph.D. thesis. Berkeley: University of California, 1950.

Dana, Julian. *The Sacramento: River of Gold*. New York: Farrar & Rinehart, 1939.

Delmatier, Royce D. *The Rumble of California Politics 1848-1970*. New York: John Wiley, 1970.

Dickman, A.I. *Interviews with Persons Involved in the Development of the Tomato Harvester*. Davis: University Library, 1978.

Dillon, Richard H. *Delta Country*. Novato: Presidio Press, 1982.

——————. *The Siskiyou Trail*. San Francisco: McGraw-Hill, 1975.

Duffy, William J., Jr. *The Sutter Basin and Its People*. Davis: The Printer, 1972.

Dunscomb, Guy L. *A Century of Southern Pacific Steam Locomotives 1862-1962*. Modesto: Dunscomb, 1963.

Fite, Gilbert C. *The Farmers' Frontier 1865-1900*. New York: Holt, Rinehart & Winston, 1966.

Giffen, Helen S. *The Diaries of Peter Decker*. Georgetown: Talisman Press, 1966.

Gilbert, Frank T. *The Illustrated Atlas and History of Yolo County*. San Francisco: DePue and Company, 1879.

Green, Will S. *The History of Colusa County and General History of the State*. Sacramento: Sacramento Lithograph Company, 1950.

Gregory, Thomas Jefferson. *History of Yolo County, California*. Los Angeles: Historic Record Company, 1913.

Gudde, Erwin Gustav. *California Place Names*. Berkeley: UC Press, 1969.

Guinn, James Miller. *History of the State of California and Biographical Record of the Sacramento Valley*. Chicago: Chapman Publishing Company, 1906.

Hafen, LeRoy and Ann W. *The Mountain Men*. Glendale: Arthur H. Clark Company, 1965-1967.

Hardwick, Susan W. "A Geographical Interpretation of Ethnic Settlement in an Urban Landscape: Russians in Sacramento." Davis: University of California at Davis, 1979.

Harlow, Neal. *California Conquered*. Berkeley: UC Press, 1982.

Heizer, Robert. "California." *Handbook of North American Indians*. Vol. 8. Washington, D.C.: Smithsonian Institution, 1978.

History of Sacramento County, California. Reproduction of Thompson & West 1880 edition. Berkeley: Howell-North Press, 1960.

History of Yolo County: A Teacher's Guide. Woodland: Yolo County Office of Education, 1964.

Hoffman's Land Cases 1853-1858. San Francisco: Numa Hubert, 1862.

Hoover, Mildred Brooke, Hero Eugene Rensch, and Ethel Grace Rensch. *Historic Spots in California*. Stanford: Stanford University Press, 1966.

Hutchison, Claude B. *California Agriculture*. Berkeley: UC Press, 1940.

Joslyn, D.L. "The Romance of the Railroads Entering Sacramento." Bulletin No. 48. Boston: Railway and Locomotive Historical Society, 1939.

Kroeber, A.S. "The Patwin and Their Neighbors." *University of California Publications in American Archaeology and Ethnology*. Vol. 29. Berkeley: UC Press, 1923.

Larkey, Joann Leach. *Davisville '68*. Davis: Davis Historical Landmarks Commission, 1969.

Lewis, Oscar. *The Big Four*. New York: Alfred A. Knopf, 1939.

McConnell, J.L. *Resources, Advantages and Prospects of Yolo County, California*. Woodland: Yolo County Board of Trade, 1887.

McGowan, Joseph A. *History of the Sacramento Valley*. New York: Lewis Historical Publishing Company, 1961.

——————, and Terry R. Willis. *Sacramento: Heart of the Golden State*. Northridge: Windsor Publications, 1983.

McKern, Willis C. "Patwin Houses." *University of California Publications in American Archaeology and Ethnology*. Vol. 20. Berkeley: UC Press, 1923.

MacMullen, Jerry. *Paddle-Wheel Days in California*. Stanford: Stanford University Press, 1944.

Memorial and Biographical History of Northern California. Chicago: Lewis Publishing Company, 1891.

Moratto, Michael. *California Archaeology*. San Diego: Academic Press, 1984.

Peninou, Ernest P. *A History of the Orleans Hill Vineyard and Winery of Arpad Haraszthy & Company*. Winters: The Winters Express, 1983.

Peterson, Edmond. "The Career of Solano, Chief of the Suisuns." Unpublished M.A. thesis. Berkeley: University of California at Berkeley, 1957.

Powers, Stephen. *Tribes of California*. Berkeley: UC Press, 1976.

Resources of Yolo County, California. Woodland: Woodland Chamber of Commerce, 1911.

Russell, William Ogburn. *History of Yolo County, California*. Woodland: 1940.

Scheuring, Ann Foley. *A Guidebook to California Agriculture by faculty and staff of the University of California*. Berkeley: UC Press, 1983.

Severson, Thor. *Sacramento: An Illustrated History, 1839 to 1874*. San Francisco: California Historical Society, 1973.

Shields, Peter J. *The Birth of an Institution*. Berkeley: Bancroft Library, 1954.

Solano, Isidora Filomena. "Narration by Isidora at Sonoma." Recorded by Henry Cerruti for H.H. Bancroft. Berkeley: Bancroft Library, 1874.

Stademan, Verne A. *The Centennial Record*. Berkeley: UC Press, 1968.

Stephens, Meredith. "The Vaca Valley and Clear Lake Railroad." Davis: University of California at Davis, 1971.

Stewart, George R. *The California Trail*. New York: McGraw-Hill, 1962.

Sutter, John A. *New Helvetia Diary*. San Francisco: Grabhorn Press, 1939.

Swett, Ira L. *Sacramento Northern*. Glendale: Interurban Press, 1981.

Taylor, Bayard. *Eldorado*. Palo Alto: Lewis Osborne, 1968.

Thompson, John, and Edward A. Dutra. *The Tule Breakers: The Story of the California Dredge*. Stockton: Stockton Corral of Westerners International, 1983.

Three Maps of Yolo County. Woodland: Yolo County Historical Society, 1970.

Transactions of the State Agricultural Society. Sacramento: State Printing Office, 1855-1919.

UC Davis: Its Development and Environment. Davis: University Farm Circle, 1980.

Walters, Shipley. *The Men and Women of the Yolanda*. Davis: University of California, 1980.

——————. *West Sacramento*. Woodland: Yolo County Historical Society, 1987.

Western Shore Gazetteer and Commercial Directory, Yolo County. Woodland: Sprague & Atwell, 1870.

Wheat, C.I. *The Maps of the California Gold Region, 1848-1857*. San Francisco: Grabhorn Press, 1942.

Wickson, E.J. "Beginnings of Agricultural Education and Research in California." Berkeley: California Agricultural Experiment Station, 1917-1919.

Wilkes, Charles. *Columbia River to the Sacramento*. Oakland: Biobooks, 1958.

Wilson, C.E. "Irrigation Investigations on Cache Creek." Washington, D.C.: USDA, 1901.

Wilson, Iris Higbie. *William Wolfskill*. Glendale: Arthur H. Clark Company, 1963.

Windows on the Past. Davis: Prytanean Society, 1984.

Winther, Oscar O. *Express and Stagecoach Days in California*. Palo Alto: Stanford University Press, 1963.

Yolo County Agriculture: Camillus Nelson State Historic Farm. Sacramento: California Department of Parks & Recreation, 1975.

Yolo in Word and Picture. Woodland: Yolo Board of Trade, 1926.

Zelinsky, Edward Galland, and Nancy Leigh Olmsted. *Upriver Boats—When Red Bluff was the Head of Navigation*. San Francisco: California Historical Society, 1985.

PRINCIPAL NEWSPAPERS

Clarksburg:
River News, 1890-date
Davis:
Davis Enterprise, 1898-date
Davisville Advertiser, 1869-1870
Esparto:
Esparto Exponent, 1913-1932
Knights Landing:
Knight's Landing News, 1859-1862
Sacramento:
Sacramento Bee, 1857-date
Sacramento Union, 1851-date
San Francisco:
Alta California, 1849-1850
West Sacramento/Broderick:
The Centinel, 1981-date
East Yolo Record, 1952-1980
Independent-Leader, 1922-1932
News-Ledger, 1964-date
Yolo Independent, 1901-1922
Winters:
Winters Advocate, 1875-1879
Winters Express, 1884-date
Woodland:
Daily Democrat, 1877-date
Home Alliance, 1891-1926
The Mail of Woodland, 1868-1937
Woodland News, 1862-1864
Woodland Record, 1938-1967
Yolo Democrat, 1864-1877

INDEX

C O L U S A   C O

T.12 N. R.3 W.   T.12 N. R.2 W.

T.11 N. R.3 W.

T.10 N. R.3 W.   T.10 N. R.2 W.

T.9 N. R.2 W.

B U C K

T.8 N. R.2 W.   T.8

S O L A N